Anxiety in Relationship

How to Overcome Couple Conflicts, Jealousy, Attachment and Insecurity in Relationship

Marta Evans

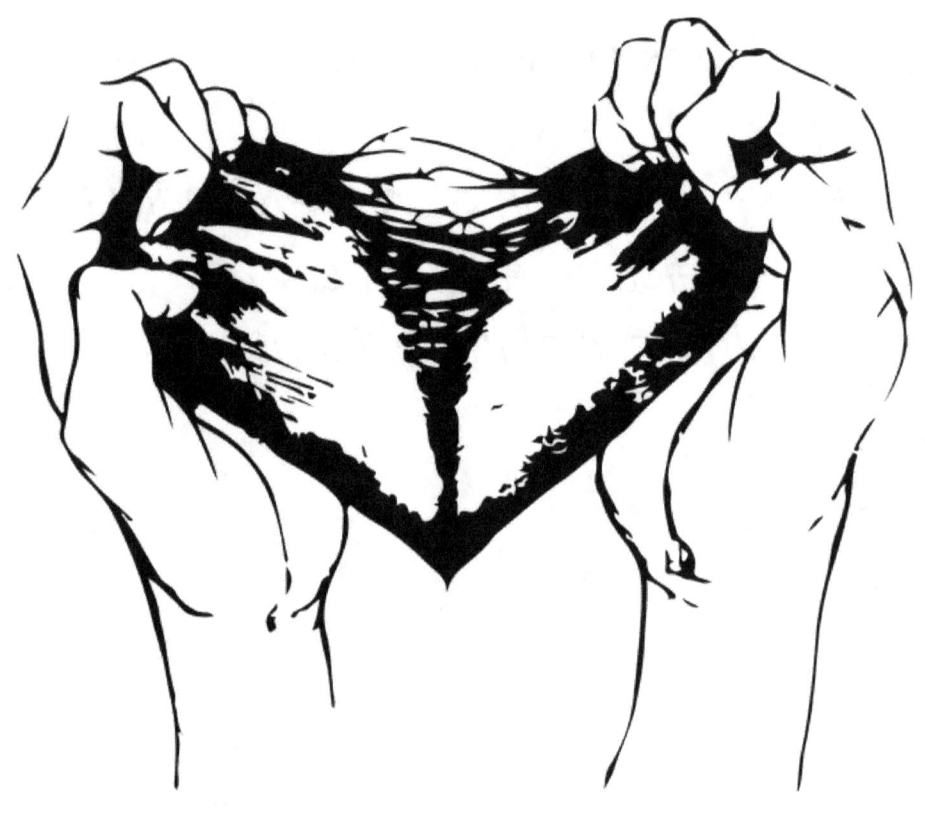

© **Copyright 2022 - All rights reserved.**

The content contained within this book may not be reproduced, duplicated, or transmitted without direct written permission from the author or the publisher.

Under no circumstances will any blame or legal responsibility be held against the publisher, or author, for any damages, reparation, or monetary loss due to the information contained within this book. Either directly or indirectly.

Legal Notice:

This book is copyright protected. This book is only for personal use. You cannot amend, distribute, sell, use, quote, or paraphrase any part, or the content within this book, without the consent of the author or publisher.

Disclaimer Notice:

Please note the information contained within this document is for educational and entertainment purposes only. All effort has been executed to present accurate, up-to-date, and reliable, complete information. No warranties of any kind are declared or implied. Readers acknowledge that the author is not engaging in the rendering of legal, financial, medical, or professional advice. The content within this book has been derived from various sources. Please consult a licensed professional before attempting any techniques outlined in this book.

By reading this document, the reader agrees that under no circumstances is the author responsible for any losses, direct or indirect, which are incurred as a result of the use of the information contained within this document, including, but not limited to, — errors, omissions, or inaccuracies.

Table of Contents:

INTRODUCTION **5**

CHAPTER 1 .... **8**
ANXIETY, NEGATIVITY AND JEALOUSY IN A RELATIONSHIP 8

CHAPTER 2 .... **44**
UNDERSTANDING COUPLE THERAPY 44

CHAPTER 3 .... **61**
IRRATIONAL BEHAVIORS IN RELATIONSHIP 61

CHAPTER 4 .... **96**
SPECIFIC PROBLEMATIC AREAS FOR COUPLES 96

CHAPTER 5 .... **128**
UNDERSTANDING EACH OTHER 128

CHAPTER 6 .... **167**
STRATEGIES TO OVERCOME ANXIETY,
NEGATIVITY, AND JEALOUSY IN A RELATIONSHIP 167

CHAPTER 7 .... **194**
SELF-EVALUATION 194

CHAPTER 8 .... **235**
HOW TO MANAGE THOUGHTS TO
CONTROL ANXIETY? 235

CONCLUSION **253**

INTRODUCTION

Anxiety is a physiological stress response that may be beneficial or harmful based on the level of the reaction. It prevents fear from being dangerous by encouraging people to deal with difficult situations. Depression is a psychological condition that may manifest itself in a variety of ways. A diligent yet depressed state of mind, a limitation of appetite and thinking, a lack of intrigue, and a variety of physical symptoms ranging from a sleeping disorder to a craving dilemma and difficult conditions are all potential causes of depression.

Depression may be brought about by a single factor or a combination of factors. Since an individual is unique, what motivates and depresses them differs as well.

However, not all experiences appropriate levels of anxiety as a result of their environment's anxious responses. Instead, certain people have intense and overwhelming responses that essentially hijack their brains and block them from rationally or reasonably processing their nervous experiences.

When you have psychiatric anxiety, the normal symptoms of your depression appear to increase significantly. Instead of a heightened yet controlled sense of fear, the symptoms appear to become unmanageable and debilitating.

Individuals with anxiety disorders are thought to have an overactive fight or flight reflex, which may lead to exaggerated responses to their original stimuli or stressor. For instance, if they have an anxiety disorder, the prospect of riding a bus alone in the city they've known their whole life can cause a full-fledged panic attack.

The possibility of going to a busy public place, on the other hand, could cause intense pain and stress symptoms such as anxiety, increased blood pressure, and intrusive thought. An anxiety condition does not always describe panic attacks, as well as the severity of the nervous response to a cause and how quickly (or not) the person is struggling to regain control of their symptoms.

While there is no clear idea of why some people experience terror in this manner, there are many reasons why some people experience anxiety.

Anxiety may be caused by an individual's anxious response to triggers that cause the memory of those difficult memories, regardless of if they have encountered something particularly unpleasant or disturbing. This kind of stimuli will often trigger PTSD, so it's vital to know whether you're dealing with actual depression or whether it's progressed to PTSD whether this is what triggered your anxiety.

Individuals' constant exposure to tension and anxiety is also thought to cause panic, which may progress to troublesome depression over time if they are unwilling to relax their minds.

This is most definitely due to prolonged sensitivity to cortisol and adrenaline, the two chemicals that cause stress and fear in those that are exposed to them. Living in a strained relationship with someone, on the other hand, will cause anyone to feel fearful all of the time, particularly if their abuser is constantly training them to be "on edge." This paranoia is exploited by an abuser who relies on their target to be scared all of the time so that they can easily throw them off balance and manipulate them more without having to fight back.

There are a variety of reasons when a person can develop anxiety, but regardless of how it manifests, problematic anxiety may be distressing and challenging to overcome. Anxiety is believed to affect more than 40 million people worldwide. Living with anxiety can be life-changing because if it becomes crippling or uncontrollable, it can negatively impact nearly every area in your life. For this reason, it is important for those suffering from anxiety to seek help in dealing with their symptoms in order to be cured and return to a normal life.

CHAPTER 1
ANXIETY, NEGATIVITY AND JEALOUSY IN A RELATIONSHIP

This chapter will introduce you to the aspects which are damaging to the relationship. It also explains the difference between the three of them and their possible solutions to overcome them or avoid them
completely.

You are partnering with a great human whom you love. You have built up trust, established limits, and learned modes of communication from each other. Around the same time, you will find yourself continuously questioning yourself, your companion, and your relationship. Would things last long? How do you decide if he's the best person for you? What if they cover up a dirty secret? And if you can't maintain a stable, dedicated relationship?

Anxiety

The deep worry has a name for itself: anxiety about relationships. This applies to certain feelings of anxiety, ambiguity, and skepticism that may occur in a relationship, even though all is going relatively well.

Is It Normal?

Relationship uncertainty is atypically natural. Some people develop relationship anxiety at the outset of a relationship until they realize that their spouse has similar values in them. Yet, they may be uncertain whether they really want a relationship. And these emotions can often occur in long-term committed relationships. Over time, concern regarding relationships will result in:

- Emotional distress
- Energy deprivation
- Depression or mental exhaustion
- Stomach discomfort and other

Physical Symptoms

The fear is not triggered by something in the relationship. And, in the end, it will contribute to acts that trigger complications and distress for you and your family.

What Are Some Signs of Relationship Anxiety?

Relationship anxiety will come up in many forms. At some point, many people feel a little uncertain about their relationship, especially in the early stages of dating and making a commitment. It's not unusual, so you don't typically have to think about passing worries or concerns, particularly if they don't bother you too much. And these tense feelings also spread and float through everyday life.

Here's a look at some possible symptoms of anxiety regarding a relationship:

Wondering if You Matter to Your Partner?

The most common type of relationship anxiety involves the essential concerns of "Do I matter? Or are you going to be there for me?" It relates to a simple desire for bonding, belonging, and feeling secure in a relationship. For example, you may be worrying that:

- Your spouse wouldn't notice you that much if you weren't around They may not be offering help or support if anything negative comes up
- They only want to be with you because of what you can do for them.

Doubting Your Partner's Feelings for You

You've expressed that I love you (or maybe I, really, like you). They are always happy when they come to see you and making nice gestures, like getting you lunch or going out of their way to see you around.

Yet the nagging doubt cannot always be shaken: "They don't really appreciate me." Or they're reluctant to react to physical affection. And, for a few hours, they don't answer texts—even a day. You wonder if their feelings changed because, unexpectedly, they appear a little detached.

From time to time, everyone thinks that way, but if you have questions regarding relationships, these feelings might become an obsession.

Worrying They Want to Break Up

A healthy relationship should make you feel affectionate, secure, and satisfied. It's completely normal to want to cling to these emotions and assume nothing can happen to ruin the relationship.

Sometimes, though, such emotions will become relentless anxiety that your companion will leave you.

This fear will become disturbing as you alter your acts to ensure their continued affection. For example, you might:

- Avoid discussing problems that are important to you in relationship, such as persistent lateness
- Ignore while your companion is doing something that annoys you, such as wearing shoes inside your home
- Stress about being angry at you, even though they don't appear upset.

Doubting Long-Term Compatibility

Anxiety about relationships will lead you to wonder that you are completely comfortable with your spouse, even if the relationship is going well. You may also inquire whether you're satisfied or whether you just look good.

In reaction, you may start concentrating your mind on small differences— they love punk music, but you are more of a folk-rock person—and overemphasizing their significance.

Sabotaging the Relationship

Sabotaging behaviors can cause anxiety in the relationship. Examples of things that could sabotage a relationship include:

- Setting up disputes with your partner pushing them away by claiming that nothing is wrong when you are under stress
- Challenging relationship expectations, such as sharing lunch with an ex without informing your spouse You do not do these actions intentionally, but the ultimate objective—whether you know it or not—is usually to know how much your spouse cares.

You might conclude, for example, that denying your efforts to push them away implies that they truly endorse you.

This is very tough for the partner to pick up on the underlying intent.

Reading Into Their Words and Actions

A propensity to overthink the partner's words and actions may often reflect concern regarding relationships.

They might not want to grasp onto their hands. And, as you take the leap and move in together, they rely on holding all their outdated furniture.

Indeed, they may all be signs of future issues. Yet, they are more likely to have sweaty palms or even like the well-set living room.

Missing Out on the Good Times

Still not sure whether you battle with relationship anxiety? Take a step back and ask yourself: "Spend more time worrying about this relationship than loving the relationship? Would this be the case in tough times? Because if you sound that way more often than not, you'll definitely be dealing with some anxiety towards relationships.

What Causes It?

It can take time to realize what's underlying your anxiety and dedicated selfexploration because there isn't just one clear cause. You can also consider it challenging to self-recognize potential causes.

"You do not recognize a source of anxiety, but regardless of how it is presented, the root causes are generally a need for interaction." Here are several important factors that may play a role.

Previous Relationship Experiences

You may tend to be affected by memories of things that have occurred in the past when you believe you've gotten through them absolutely.

You might be more prone to develop relationship anxiety if a previous spouse:

- Betrayed you
- Unexpectedly abandoned you lied regarding their feelings towards you exploited you about the nature of your relationship

It's not unusual to have problems having trust in someone again when you've been hurt—particularly though the new relationship doesn't exhibit any symptoms of manipulation or dishonesty.

Any trigger, whether you know it or not, will also remind you of the past and trigger doubts and insecurities.

Low Self-Esteem

Low self-esteem may also contribute to relationship instability and anxiety. Some older research suggests that people with lower self-esteem are more prone to question their partner's feelings while experiencing self-doubt. This will happen as a type of projection.

In other terms, feeling insecure in yourself can make things harder for you to accept that you feel likewise about your partner.

By contrast, people with greater self-esteem tended to help themselves while they encountered self-doubt in their relationship.

Attachment Style

The attachment style you establish during childhood may have a major impact on our adult relationships.

If your parent or caregiver actively answered your concerns and gave affection and encouragement, you've already developed a healthy type of attachment.

If they have not fulfilled your needs regularly or encouraged you to develop individually, then your attachment style will be less secure.

Insecure attachment types can relate in a variety of ways to anxiety regarding relationships:

- Resisting attachment can lead to anxiety about the degree of commitment you create or intensify intimacy.
- Anxious attachment, on the other side, will also contribute to fears that your companion may unexpectedly leave you.

Bear in mind that getting an insecure personality style does not imply you're destined to still feel anxious for relationships.

Because you can't move your relationship style from one form of personality to another, then you can't totally alter it, so ideally, you will make enough changes where a dysfunctional sort of commitment won't keep you down in life—a tendency to question.

A skeptical attitude can be another factor of anxiety regarding relationships.

Until you decide on a path, you might need to remind yourself of all possible interpersonal consequences. And maybe you're already getting used to taking every decision carefully.

When you decide to ask yourself some questions regarding your choices, you would possibly spend some time challenging your relationship, too, long after you have made them. This isn't always a problem. In fact, it is usually safer to take time to reflect on choices you made, particularly significant ones (like romantic engagement).

But, if you find yourself stuck in a constant loop of confusion and self-doubt that does not go forward somewhere, it may become a problem.

When one or both individuals in the relationship invest most energy thinking about the relationship than going into the relationship itself." "Fear of rejection, feeling as if they matter most, incessant fear of infidelity, or a general mistrust of the relationship's continuity leads to a loss of faith.

There are many factors you might be worried about regarding the relationship; two manipulative spouses set the stage early on in adult life for future issues. Emotional relationships are also used as threats to parents, violent exes, inadequate communication, and unsuccessful counseling. Of starters, self-help books on relationships may often encourage elusive, distant, and unexplained acts in holding a spouse hooked. "None of these issues promote a stable, reliable relationship." A person with insecurity regarding relationships doesn't inherently have an untrustworthy spouse. If you don't express your worries and expectations, your significant companion can well simply live their life, totally oblivious of your problems. Any conduct that allows one spouse to distrust the other at the same time generates conflict. Relationship problems blow up when compared to posts on social media. "The game of competition and contrast fosters insecurity that your relationship isn't as successful as some, which allows pessimistic thoughts to develop when you ruminate that your relationship isn't as 'healthy' as others." That's, of course, just speculation.

Relationship Anxiety Is a Two-Person Problem
If you have anxiety about relationships, it will definitely be your first impulse to cover it up—especially if you know that your fears are actually overblown. Above all, no one needs to behave intensely for no reason or appears to be overbearing. Yet this is the interesting thing about anxiety: while it is often experienced

solely by one person in the relationship, it is the concern of both spouses.

If you're an anxious partner, your task is to discuss as quickly as possible what's bothering you and why. Does the apprehension find its origins in the baggage of the past? The anxious person needs to be able to accurately perceive the concerns. You don't feel like you've been desired, needed, appreciated, or have been the only one? Is the connection lacking an emotionally intimate bond? Is the connection lacking physically intimate contact? That is when a companion of an individual falls short. Anxiety can be challenging to place in words; it sounds disordered, frenzied, and disturbed.

When you are ever unsure about the relationship, here is the formula: Discover the source of the anxiety, explain the trigger to your partner and suggest a fix. "When a partner understands where the anxiety originates, it's easier to come to terms about. On top of this, there would be no dilemma without a solution. Ask them when you think you'd be happier. You may need reassurance, and you may like them to be less vigilant with how they're writing—giving your partner insight into your feelings. Whether you're not worried because your spouse does, you will probably benefit from it. That includes listening carefully, asking questions, always being honest, and speaking more often than you might find necessary.

Negativity

Negativity may also come in the form of cynicism, critique, moaning, bullying, pessimism, deceit, perfectionism, and hyper-intensity. Any of these practices will scare away people, including your spouse.

Are You Naturally Negative?

If you're nervous about having or leaning on a negative attitude side, then ask yourself the following questions.

- Do you fall into an unpleasant mood quite often? Do you focus on negative or upsetting thoughts?
- Are you dismissive of everyone in your life? Look at incidents and occurrences from a pessimistic point of view?
- Are you a perfectionist? When somebody says, "Good morning," do you question what a good thing is?

Are you eager to say "no" to your partner or kids and never say' yes? 'When you respond yes to any of these questions, your pessimistic attitude might potentially impact your relationship.

Change Your Pattern of Negativity

If you're consistently pessimistic, you can change your pessimistic thinking pattern. You need to make this adjustment, though, and nobody can do it for you.

Here are a few more helpful things you should do:

- Eat a balanced diet
- Carry in some compassion
- Get enough sleep
- Willing to forgive oneself and their kin
- Practice patience
- Physical activity

Do something every single day to make yourself content. Simply listen to a favorite song, spend time on an artistic project, enjoy an interesting video, or take a bubble bath

If you sense a negative reaction flowing into your head, question this. Then try to think of something positive.

- Volunteer and collaborate with others
- Keep in contact with fellow optimists
- Think of things you're really thankful for
- Praise the partner anytime a good situation occurs, such as effectively finishing a difficult work project
- Be open to finding professional assistance

Help Your Negative Spouse

When you are in a relationship with a person who has a negative mindset, helping them feel comfortable is not your obligation. Yet these are few measures that you should do to make your partner feel more positive:

- Don't take the criticism personally
- Know the negativity is their dilemma and not yours
- Should not overreact if your companion rejects your supportive bid Spend time with positive people. You would be willing to take some time out from the stress and negativity at home
- Invite your mate to take a walk or do something fun with you, at least once a week

- Consider the achievements the individual has accomplished
- Inspire your partner to seek something new
- Don't dream about saying "Enough!" and changing the topic to anything more optimistic

Be opened to getting professional support

Turn the Negative into Positive

Overall, bear in mind Dr. Gottman's advice: Build five positives for each negative. Often, it can be a challenge, and there is no ideal relationship or marriage. Yet having fun, being open to dialogue, and loving one another are some of the keys to a happy and safe marriage.

Try the best you can to seek to overcome the negativity you feel. Over time, you might be amazed at the impact it has on both of you.

Sings of Negativity

Negative Energy

You get so tensed, agitated, and frustrated with your partner while you engage in a toxic relationship that you build up negative energy in your body and later lead to absolute hatred towards each other.

Negativity can rob you in all aspects of your life. Negativity destroys you on an intellectual, physical, personal, moral, and intellectual basis. We are expected to deal with this misery, but that form of stress should be a release from your negative relationship.

You Are Not Just Happy Being in the Relationship

Another important indication of a negative relationship is you're not just content anymore. We all realize that at any moment of your life, you can't be perfect, but your spouse can always make you better as a whole. He or she can make you feel secure, dedicated, contented, and ready to do anything you want. This is an alert sign that if you are not feeling positive about your mate, you are in a negative relationship.

You Don't Trust Your Partner

If you don't trust your partner anymore, that is a clear indication of a negative relationship. You're in a destructive relationship when you start questioning your partner's behavior and actions.

When your partner just twists the facts if they don't like the way a conversation is going, it's an indicator you're involved in a relationship with a person that isn't trustworthy. It means you are in a toxic relationship with an untrustworthy individual when your spouse accuses someone else of their actions, or any sort of flimsy circumstances, for their liability.

You Don't Communicate Effectively

Much as communication is the very essence of a relationship that is healthy and effective, its lack implies that the relationship is destructive, unhealthy, toxic, and is about to perish. You don't speak to each other face to face, even though you are with each other. You prefer the usage of gestures and texts rather than verbal communication.

You won't be able to interact successfully in a negative relation. That means you don't even have much to say to your partner anymore. If something occurs in life, whether it's an achievement, an accident, or an event and your partner isn't the first one you're discussing everything with- that's a clear indication of a negative relation.

You Are Not Connected to Each Other

If you do not like being in the company of your partner, it is an indication that you are in a negative or toxic relationship. When you're together, but not really together, it's a clear indication of a negative and incompatible relationship. You may be in the same place; however, one of you is reading, or you are on your phone. You may not feel related to another person even though you both sleep together in the same room.

You are always together because you realize that you never actively communicate with each other; rather, you do your own thing; instead, that is an indication that you no longer relate to each other. Which indicates you are involved in a destructive relationship.

You Feel Insecure

If you start feeling uncomfortable in a relationship and don't know your place in a relationship, it obviously shows you are in a negative relationship.

You may feel like; you don't know where you stand or contribute to in a relationship. That is, you are feeling insecure, unsure, or anxious about the relationship's future.

When you're beginning to feel insecure and unsure about a relationship, speak to your partner, and explore where the two of you are heading in the relationship. If he or she cannot provide you with a suitable response or explanation, please get back out of the relationship. Such a relationship is negative, toxic, and destructive, split up, and try as much as possible to avoid the relationship.

Jealousy

Although feeling jealous is something that anyone can relate to, the feeling is often mistaken with envy. Yet envy and jealousy are very distinct. Envy is a response to something that's lacking and a longing for something someone has. They can envy somebody's good looks, or their lovely home, etc. On the other side, the belief that anyone may try to steal what is yours is jealousy. For example, with an attractive co-worker, your husband is fast buddies, and you might feel jealous of their relationship—and disturbed by it.

In its mildest jealousy, it's called an instinctual response that makes us want to defend what we know is ours. While only being territorial, though, jealous feelings can quickly turn into disruptive acts and lead us to behave in narcissistic and manipulating ways. This may even push one to assume stuff that doesn't exist, like interpreting a casual interaction as the indication of adultery or working late as keeping a dark addiction.

Jealousy is either instinctual or not, and it's unproductive. People dealing with manipulative, jealous feelings are often frequently grappling with more profound issues. Uncontrolled jealous acts are typically a sign of one or more of the following:

- Insecurity
- Fear
- Low self-esteem

Either of these three or a combination will not only express a sense of jealousy in disruptive behavior but may also cause certain issues in a person's life.

What Jealousy Does to Your Relationship?

Jealous behavior may destroy a relationship. For best, the jealous spouse becomes insecure and deliberately seeks reassurance that they are the only one and that there is no one to substitute them. Controlling and distrustful attitude, and even physical or emotional aggression, can manifest jealously at its worst.

A jealous partner can seek to control the behavior of their partner, check their locations, or monitor their calls, texts, or emails. Such conduct produces an unhealthy habit of mistrust, which eventually contributes to the deterioration of a relationship.

Trust and respect are the solid foundation of a secure and happy relationship. A person dealing with jealousy cannot trust or display affection for the person he or she is with as an individual or his or her boundaries.

Over time this activity would destroy feelings of love and intimacy that once occurred. It will undoubtedly also cause frequent fights and one person's ability to assert themselves and their honesty over and over again. This may be comprehensive and preclude the formation of a relationship and the creation of a stable foundation.

How Can You Control It?

Management of jealous behavior can be difficult. The root issues never all go down on their own. If jealousy is a regular pattern of behavior that is repeated in a relationship after another one, it may require the guidance of a skilled psychiatrist to both reins in it and offer support to cope with the causes that fuel it.

In a relationship going past jealousy means building faith. One spouse must be confident enough in the other to know that the love and affection they share will deter outside influences from disrupting their relationship, irrespective of the circumstances. It can be difficult when one person becomes insecure and usually struggles with trust.

When you have learned that jealousy is a problem in your relationship, whether you are insecure or your partner, it may be tough for you all; going above this will require patience, coordination, and belief shift. If it doesn't suit to overcome competitive feelings and behavior, don't ignore finding support.

Jealousy is one of the most prevalent emotions among all feelings. You get jealous anytime you know you're going to lose a relationship you really trust. It often adds to tense and mistrustful behaviors that strike men and women with similar rage. Unfortunately, with age, it does not appear to mellow.

Types of Jealousy

There are two very different forms of jealousy: Reactive jealousy and suspicious jealousy; this difference is important since nearly everyone experiences reactive jealousy when one knows that a spouse has been unfaithful. But individuals vary in their tendency to experience suspicious jealousy in the absence of any direct threat.

Reactive Jealousy

Reactive jealousy occurs when a couple, for example, is aware of a possible obstacle or risk to the relationship when one of the spouses learns that the other person was potentially unfaithful. There is often some sort of jealousy in reaction to a realistic threat.

Suspicious Jealousy

While the jealousy is suspicious as the spouse has not misbehaved, no sign is provided that a marital partner has engaged in some actions that may significantly, perhaps even legally, impact the relationship's stability. You sit at a restaurant, for example, and you notice that your companion is smiling at an attractive woman across the way. A victim of suspicious jealousy may interpret such a gesture as a threat to the status of the relationship and may become angry with the partner for flirting with the stranger. This is too frequently the case in books, film, and television. This form of jealousy is sometimes followed by a slap in the face or two partners arguing over the suspicions.

How to Overcome Jealousy

Be Honest

If your partner has a valid cause to be jealous, then it might be time to have a heart-to-heart discussion regarding the future of the relationship.

Build Self-Confidence

It's crucial to understand that signs of jealousy cannot have much to do with you or your actions. If your partner does not have a legitimate basis for jealousy, the presence of jealous feelings indicates that your partner may suffer from a lack of trust. They may be confused about their own situation in any aspect. Encourage your companion to spend time with relatives and colleagues who believe they are great or learn something new.

Gain Independence

There might also be jealousy as couples depend too much on the relationship to determine how they feel regarding themselves and their self-worth. Convince them to choose to become more independent from you and the relation. The less competitive, the more they attribute their self-definition to their own achievements and encounters away from the relationship. Envy may be almost as detrimental to relationships as the two types of jealousy.

Listen Carefully

Do not disregard your partner's feelings and anxieties. It might not have been convenient for the partner to fess up and express his or her thoughts or doubts. This also makes the person feel powerless and not in control. We have always had times like that. Try to understand, empathize, and, if you may listen. If jealousy arises during the early stages of a relationship you'd like to protect, it's cool to be there to comfort your partner when he or she hits the depths of what's causing those feelings of jealousy. At the same time, the adjustments that need to develop will be coming from inside the person.

Seek Assistance

Insecurity may be cured easily as, in reality, it is essentially "cosmetic." (For example, if the female partner says she might be more confident if she shed a few pounds.) Furthermore, other symptoms of jealousy, such as those culminating in aggressive behavior, may be a symptom of greater distress and are treated best with the aid of a therapist.

Jealousy tends to destroy the base on which to create stable relationships. It is necessary to remember that, overnight, they will not build stable foundations. That's one significant reality.

Misjudgment That Jealousy Is a Symbol of Love Is Popular

Jealousy may be a major relationship concern—a survey undertaken by relational therapists found that a third of their clients perceived romantic jealousy as a severe problem. They ought to dissipate the misjudgment that jealousy is a sign of love. Yet if not, what motivates these jealous responses then? Studies also associated many characteristics with greater jealousy:

Low self-esteem

Neuroticism: A general propensity to be moody, anxious, and emotionally disturbed

- **Feels low and possessive**
- **Dependence on your mate:** Only asking people to consider struggling to find a good substitute relationship contributes to more negative reactions to hypothetical jealousy-causing scenarios
- **Feelings of inadequacy in your relationship:** Typically worried your spouse is not going to be good enough
- **An inappropriate attachment style:** A pervasive attitude toward romantic relationships that involves fear that your spouse may or may not value you sufficiently. Research has found that briefly allowing people to feel more strongly connected by encouraging them to think about having support from a loved one makes them react less negatively to a hypothetical, jealousy-inducing situation

All of these factors which lead to jealousy are about the insecurities of the jealous people, not about the love of their partner for them.

So, what do you do when unjustified jealousy is expressed by your mate?

You should be certain that your partner's jealousy isn't about you; it's about them. Respond to jealousy expressions by reassuring your love for your partner. Evidence has found that those who respond by assuring them of their worth and appeal to partners' jealousy tend to have more stable relationships.

What Should You Do if You're Jealous?

How do you deal with jealousy if you are the one who snoops into the emails of your partner? There are some acts that will help you cope:

- **Avoid conditions that could trigger false suspicions.** In one analysis, researchers observed that those who were jealous tended to watch their partners' Facebook activities. The more they sneak into your Facebook or other social media account, the more facts they'd find complaining about, resulting in even greater surveillance and a vicious cycle of intensified control and jealousy.

- **Work on your own.** Concentrate on strengthening self-confidence and relationship.

- **Let your partner know.** When you're feeling jealous, speak about it to your spouse—but the way you're communicating about it is key: if you're expressing rage or sarcasm or hurling accusations at your partner, it won't help. You need to be straightforward but not aggressive. Respectfully clarify your thoughts and discuss means of finding a solution. It will make you feel more comfortable with your negative behavior and avoid disappointing your partner. These coping strategies are more apt to give the friend supportive reactions.

Jealousy is also justified because, for example, your wife has an affair and compromised your trust, which is a serious issue. When you're upset that you're interacting with someone who doesn't want monogamy when you're doing it, so your insecure emotions might be a legitimate reason to leave the relationship and find someone that's more compatible with your desires for your relationship. Yet when you get jealous of "stupid stuff," you don't display much love; you reveal your own insecurities.

It tips jealousy over its head. Jealousy is now an opportunity to interact in relationships rather than one to avoid. Vulnerability is the cradle of love, belonging, happiness, bravery, empathy, and inspiration. It is where optimism, kindness, accountability, and integrity come from. "We will do so in a careful and constructive manner because we recognize that we are jealous. Recognizing and acknowledging the partner's innate flaws and you can strengthen the relationship.

Understand Your Triggers

Jealousy within a relationship may be more about your own flaws than about your mate's actions. Of starters, if you have endured tragedy in your life, you may be prone to jealousy. It is important to speak to your spouse about these experiences because you can be conscious of each other's triggers and accept them.

Jealousy may be steered by low self-esteem or a negative self-perception. When you do not feel comfortable and secure, it may be challenging to honestly accept that you value your spouse and trust them. Many times, unreasonable expectations may cause jealousy about the relationship. It's not healthy for couples to spend 100 percent of their time together. Remember, the feelings aren't true. Let the pessimistic thoughts float free. Recognize them before expelling them deliberately.

Emotions of jealousy will become problematic if they influence the acts and emotions about the relationship as a whole. Below are some of the signs of sinister jealous behavior.

- Check your spouse's phone or email without authorization
- Insult your spouse
- Presume your spouse isn't attracted to you
- Harass your spouse at their place of residence all day long
- Accuse your spouse of deception without evidence

If you find either of these patterns in your relationship, try and clarify the vulnerabilities.

Use Jealousy for Good

Jealousy may also be a very real and rational response to the partner's behavior in a relationship. Remember that people have high expectations for how they are treated in a relationship that is good enough. They look forward to love, compassion, affection, and appreciation. They turn to their mate for fidelity and integrity.

When the reaction is, "Is that so?" "Yeah, so asking your partner how you feel when the jealousy becomes frustration is important. Keep to the" I "phrases as you bring it up and avoid saying stuff like" you do "or" you never. "Talk about your thoughts towards the particular circumstance and making broad conclusions regarding your partner's character. Say what you need and not what you do not. For example, I feel nervous because, when you are out, I don't know where you are or who you are with. I need you to give me an update and let me know. "The better the relationship will be, the more you speak. Is there a specific arrangement that makes you uncomfortable? Do you find that you're stonewalled or that the spouse's behavior has changed recently? You and your spouse will be open regarding relationships and working arrangements with each other and out front. "If it hurts, then it reaches a mark. Show each other how much you value each other by placing your relationship ahead of your profession, your colleagues, and your buddies. You develop trust every time you do that. By understanding what controls your feelings and acknowledging each other's endearing flaws, you will leverage jealousy for the best.

Jealousy is a tangle of thoughts and feelings caused by perceived threats to a relationship, and it gets a bad reputation because of how certain people respond when it reaches them; it's harmful if it acts violently, but if it's treated as a force for good it can be a useful signal.

Welcome Reminder

The immediate sting of jealousy can prompt you to demonstrate how valuable your partner is to you. "The bond may be complicated by jealousy; we always require a nudge to remember what is really important, so use the feeling as an excuse to simply express the love for your partner.

Communication Booster

If you think of it, jealousy tends to reinforce the relationship. "The trick is an effective conversation rather than bottling in the jealousy and letting it come out in unhelpful, passive-aggressive forms – like 'I'm sorry I haven't got a body like that girl who was flirting with you all night at the party. Rather, she advises being assertive and saying something like this," I have to admit you, I've got a little insecure seeing that gorgeous lady flirt with you tonight. You look amazing.

Aphrodisiac

Being riled up at the thought of someone snagging your sweetie may be a potent sign that the physical attraction is either alive—or in control. "It will allow us to see from fresh eyes and rediscover the positive attributes that drew us in the first place," A person we lost confidence in is even more appealing immediately when another woman flirts with him, which can contribute to a precious, revived flame. You must not wait to act upon such feelings.

Goal Fuel

Jealousy causes you to be disappointed with some aspect of yourself, which can be all the motivation you need to take constructive action to change it. For example, "A woman was insecure because of her husband's beautiful and physically healthy coworker. Unhappy with the way she felt in her own body, she was attempting to shed those extra pounds to get the body she needed," the result? It is something the client and her partner will definitely appreciate.

Motivation to Be Better Half

At times we all get distracted or sluggish, so we might catch ourselves slacking off on our part of the relationship. "Jealousy may be an encouragement to be the greatest partner you can be but use it to prove how much it means to you. You should surprise him with a meal that you realize he likes or tickets to see his favorite movie. Renewed commitment can" change the relationship and inspire him to become an even better partner.

Insecurity Radar

Feeling jealous can lead to deeper hang-ups, so listen to the warning signs and get to the real problem. You can reflect on your "experience with jealousy and realize whether it derives from a feeling of being inferior, whether it emerges from adolescence, or you might notice that jealousy comes from a fundamental difference in the relationship, one person becoming far more interested than the other." If so, start thinking about ways you may fix such problems, whether it involves counseling or heart-to-heart with your partner or both of these.

Attention Tune-Up

It is all too easy for our strained attention to drift away from our most important relationship. No worries – just take notice and take action. "A jealous person found that she was more excited about her children than she was about her husband. To fix this, she purposely offered her husband a huge embrace and kissed him anytime she left or returned home. This improved the terms of their relationship.

The Gift of Mutual Reassurance

Think about it this way: When you feel jealous, it is really obvious how satisfying reassurance can be. In other terms, you want your man to tell, "There's nothing to be jealous about. You're everything to me." What you didn't even know is that he feels comfortable because you're honest with your feelings, too. "For him, there is the reassurance that you love sufficiently to be jealous and respect the relationship enough to step up your game. Everyone likes to feel loved and appreciated.

CHAPTER 2

UNDERSTANDING COUPLE THERAPY

This chapter discusses how to grasp couples counseling from both angles. You will also get an understanding of how couples counseling works in couples' favor. Both facets of how couple counseling acts as a helpful
source for reconnecting partners, as well as the whole phenomenon behind it, are explored in-depth in each chapter below.

What Is Couple Therapy?

Couples that are married or engaged to each other will benefit from counseling. This is often referred to as family counseling. The aim of pair counseling is to help couples strengthen and deepen their relationships. Couples may use this type of therapy to decide if they can be together or not. There are times that either or both partners ought to talk about their psychological issues separately.

Understanding

Sessions aimed at improving problem-solving, building coping skills, and setting life objectives and standards for relationships are often used in therapy. Infidelity, financial challenges, sickness, and other life transitions, as well as dissatisfaction, are all common issues.

Depending on the severity of the relationship's problems, counseling should be done in a brief amount of time or for multiple months. If you and your wife are having issues because you still wind up in a huge fight whenever you argue, and nothing gets fixed. Thanks to the high level of stress in your relationship, the two of you are increasingly drifting apart. You've always considered quitting your wife, so you'd like to pursue pair counseling first.

You're in therapy because you've realized that you need help with both your interpersonal skills and your problem-solving strategies. You often realize that you are just repeating your parents' actions, which was to scream and do little before finally falling apart and divorcing. With your newfound understanding that part of the problem is that you mimic what your parents do, you will now adjust your conduct. You use positive coping techniques and a workable problem approach to improve the relationship over time. Positive emotions for your wife resurface, and you'll find it difficult to believe you decided to end the engagement.

Five Principles of Effective Couple Therapy

Five basic principles of effective couple's therapy are as follows:

Changes the Views of the Relationship

Throughout the counseling phase, the therapist seeks to assist both sides in seeing the relationship in a more realistic light. They learn to stop playing the "blame role" and instead focus on what happens to them in a loop that involves all spouses. It's, therefore, a good idea to make sure their friendship occurs in a particular way. Couples that are struggling financially, for example, can be subjected to various types of situational tension than others who are not. Therapists initiate this phase by watching how the couples interact to collect "information" regarding their relationship. The therapists then develop "hypotheses" regarding what causes may be contributing to the issues in the couple's relationship. Therapists communicate their experience with couples based on the therapist's fundamental psychological viewpoint, which ranges from couple to couple. There is scientific evidence for a variety of approaches, from therapeutic to insight oriented. Different therapists can take different methods, but as long as they focus on strengthening the pair's view of each other and their perceptions, the couple may continue to perceive each other and their experiences in a more positive light.

Modifies Dysfunctional Behavior

Good couple therapists try to improve the way the partners actually communicate with one another. In addition to helping them enhance their relationship, this means that therapists do need to ensure that their clients do not participate in behaviors that can cause physical, psychological, or economic damage.

To do so, therapists must carry out a detailed evaluation to decide if their clients are genuinely at risk. For example, if possible, the therapist may recommend that one person be sent to a shelter for domestic violence, a specialist clinic for substance abuse, or anger management. It is also likely that if the risk isn't serious enough, the couple can benefit from "time-out" measures to avoid conflict escalation.

Decreases Emotional Avoidance

Couples that refrain from sharing their private feelings are at greater risk of being emotionally isolated and growing apart. Efficient couple therapists help their clients put out the feelings and ideas they are unable to convey to others. Couple counseling based on intimacy helps couples to feel less anxious to communicate their desire for closeness. According to this view, some partners in childhood who have failed to build "free" emotional attachments have unmet needs that they bring into their adult relationships. They are afraid to show their partners how much they need them because they are afraid their partners are going to reject them. Behavioral therapists believe that adults may be unable to communicate their true feelings because they have not received "reinforcement" in the past. Either way, all psychological strategies recommend encouraging their clients to convey their true feelings in a way that would ultimately bring them back together.

Improves Communication

Intimacy is one of the "three C's" of being able to communicate. All positive couple therapies are geared towards helping the couples connect more effectively. Building on concepts 2 and 3, this contact should not be violent, nor will partners make one another crazy as they share their true feelings. Therefore, couples can need "coaching" in order to learn to talk to one another in a more supportive and understanding way. The therapist can also give instructional advice to the couple and provide them with the basis for understanding what forms of communication are successful, and what forms would only create more tension. For example, they could learn how to listen more actively and empathetically. Just how to achieve this step, however, allows therapists to switch back to the tests they carried out early in care. Couples with a persistent history of mutual criticism can involve an approach different from those who seek to avoid confrontation at all costs.

Promote Strengths

Good couple therapists point out the strengths of the relationship and develop resilience, particularly when therapy is about to end. Since so much couple counseling includes concentrating on problem areas, it's easy to lose sight of the other areas where the couple work effectively. Promoting strength is about helping the couple gain more satisfaction from their relationship. The behaviorally focused therapist can "prescribe" one partner to do something agreeable to another. Perhaps therapists from other orientations who concentrate more on feelings may help the couple create a more optimistic "plot" or narrative about their relationship. In this case, the therapist should stop trying to put his or her own perspective on what constitutes a strength and let the couple determine this.

We can see, then, that if their life seems hopeless, people in strained relationships need not give up in despair. In the same way, people who are reluctant to enter into long-term relationships will be motivated to learn how to repair problem relationships.

Looking at the other side, these five concepts of good counseling recommend strategies for partners to develop healthy close relationships and sustain them. Take an unbiased look at your relationship, seek assistance in eliminating unhealthy habits, feel like you can express your feelings, connect openly, and show what works. Most importantly, by ensuring that each relationship has its own specific challenges and strengths, you can give yours the best survival chances.

How Does Couple Therapy Work?

Counseling will benefit couples with the use of the above approaches and more. For couple counseling to succeed, both people must be committed to enhancing their relationship while looking inwardly at their own strengths and weaknesses. Knowing their behaviors and habits that make your partner tick could have a positive impact on making improvements in both personal aspects and relationships. Couple's therapy is not intended to unload anger, frustration, and other negative actions against one spouse. It's about finding passion, commitment, and all the other approaches that lead to a healthy relationship.

Does marriage counseling work? That's a very big issue, but what people are really talking about is, "Will marriage therapy save my marriage? The response to that is very much based on a variety of variables beyond the counselor's office.

Although some of these points are highlighted below, some of the considerations to look for when seeking marital therapy are as follows:

- Did you just wait too long? If you have been breaking each other apart for ten years, there is a very good risk that there is so much harm that it cannot be done to undo.
- Need to save your marriage? People often go to therapy just to claim they've tried. They just don't want it to work. They save face just to assuage their remorse.
- Is there harassment or aggression in the relationship? If there is a family, you're not trying to save it; you're trying to avoid the illegal activity.
- Abusers, whether physical or mental, are not "unhappy" in their marriage; they are often terrified and impotent people who feel helpless in their lives anywhere else.
- Will the structure meet your needs? If saving your marriage means spending another 30 years doing away with everything you want to do, is that worth it? It takes a hard and truthful look at what every person needs to make sure you get exactly that what you need out of the relationship.

One of the most important factors in relationship counseling's success is the counselor. Nearly every counselor in the world claims they're doing marital therapy, but most never received any preparation. They also have a psychology or counseling degree and believe they should do it.

Marriage therapy is not about one person and their problems. There are two individuals, their problems, and the relationship and dynamics of these things.

Marriage therapy is not just therapy—it's an advanced talent that requires a specialist.

Statistics Show High Rates of Patient Satisfaction

There are high rates of patient satisfaction demonstrated by families and couples who attended family or couple counseling sessions. Over 98 percent of the surveys reported having received good or excellent couple counseling, and more than 97 percent said they had the support they wanted. 93 percent of clients, having met with a marriage or family therapist, said they had more powerful resources to cope with their problems. Respondents have indicated improved physical health after completing therapy and the ability to perform better at work.

Marriage or Family Counseling Consumes Less Time Than Individual Counseling

If you ask yourself, "does marriage therapy work?" The response can depend on whether your partner is willing or not to go with you to therapy. When your partner refuses to go with you to therapy, you will change the dynamics of your relationship only by going to individual counseling. Statistics, however, indicate that couples or family therapy are typically faster and more effective than a single therapy alone. If a couple or a family goes together to counseling, they have the ability to focus on the dynamics of their community, and this leads them to more rapid results. Usually, reaching a target in the family or couple therapy takes about one-third fewer sessions than it does in individual therapy. This means you're going to spend less money and get your marriage back on track faster than if you're only trying to help out.

Emotionally Focused Therapy Works

Here exists no magical cure that can repair a broken relationship, but many therapists have had great success using the Emotionally Focused Therapy or EFT method of therapy. When asked, "Does therapy work in marriage?" Statistics show that when couples use EFT, the answer is usually yes. EFT works by helping a person understand their emotional reactions to events and reorganize them. Working with their emotional cycles will give a couple a deeper understanding of each other, and this can help them build new relationship cycles. Ninety percent of them record major changes in their relationship when couples turn to EFT. Between 70 and 75 percent of depressed couples will switch to recovery using EFT. EFT basically lets a couple foster their relationship safely and successfully.

Couples Therapy Works Better When Couples Seek for Help Early

Sadly, there are no clear statistics to support this claim, but therapists usually assume the answer to "does marriage therapy work? "And most often when the couple seeks counseling at the earliest possible moment. When a couple waits until their issues are too far advanced, one person might already have given up on the relationship, and it may be difficult to save the relationship at that stage. For other situations, contact habits have been so aggressive or hostile that the therapist may be unable to teach the couple new strategies for contact. The couples will pursue counseling as soon as possible for the best chance of success. Even couples may wish to sign up for premarital counseling.

Degrees May Not Matter Much; It Is More Important to Find a Therapist Who Is Right for You

Statistics show that it does not matter how much knowledge the marriage therapist has. A poll of 4,000 respondents found that irrespective of whether they saw a psychologist, therapist, or social worker, people feel the same about their therapy.

Researchers felt the treatment was less successful in situations where patients only had a small range of options because of limitations imposed by their insurance provider. Since the effectiveness levels of various mental health providers seem to vary very little, you may simply want to select your therapist based on your intuition. If it sounds like you could be assisted by a specific therapist, then schedule a session. If not, then speak to another expert.

Marriage Counseling Requires Shopping Around

Surveys show that in private practice, about eighty percent of therapists do pair therapy. How they got their training is a mystery because most therapists working today have never taken a few counseling courses and have never done their internships under the guidance of someone who perfected the craft. In the point of view of a person going in for a couple, therapy is like getting your broken leg fixed by a doctor who missed orthopedics in medical school. It's important not to just pick someone nearby or even someone who has a degree, to look for someone who has been qualified in marriage counseling. Ask them, look up their qualifications online, and ask for feedback from other therapists. Has marriage therapy ever been fully educated in marital counseling with the person doing the counseling? Not much and not very often.

The Pain of Breakup Needs to Outweigh the Pain of Marriage

Change happens when the pain of remaining the same is greater than the pain of change. It may sound like a strange assertion, but it's real. Most of us don't find divorce less difficult than remaining together; however, it can be. There are few factors that can cause pain in marriage. Consider if breaking up is not what's best for you, the family, and the other person when contemplating therapy (and that can be the number one conversation with a great counselor).

One wants to believe it, but there are moments when it was a mistake to get married, and it is something you can reverse. If you've built a life, though, started a family, and shared years together, that's a decision that needs to be taken with sensitivity.

If your marriage has ended or is on the rocks and you know a couple who have recently married or are considering it, persuade them to get therapy now. They shouldn't wait for their marriage to fall apart. Much as you go to a doctor every year, constantly focusing on it will look to keep your marriage safe. Was marital therapy successful in this case? Yes. Especially when it comes to getting it when you need it the most.

Couple Therapy as a Beneficial Source to Reconnect

Couple counseling will benefit couples with the use of the above approaches and more. For couple counseling to succeed, all parties need to be committed to strengthening their relationship while looking inwardly at their own strengths and weaknesses. Knowing their behaviors and habits that make your partner tick could have a positive impact on making improvements in both personal and relationship aspects. Couple counseling is not intended to unload anger, frustration, and other negative habits to one spouse. It's about finding passion, commitment, and all the other approaches that go into a good relationship.

The couple's therapist looks into the ins and outs of the relationship between the couple and gives them insight into their mutual strengths and weaknesses as well as their personalities. The therapist serves as a neutral mediator and gives all partners advice. He or she can encourage more two-way contact, build more constructive ways of communicating and thinking, and multiple ways the couple can show each other their affection and support while in the therapy process.

Couple therapy, in any case, does not benefit everyone; many people still express their concern for couple therapy and methods of reconnecting with their spouse. Many of the advantages of combination therapy include:

High Levels of Satisfaction

Couples show higher levels of satisfaction and overall happiness during counseling sessions and then afterward. Ninety-seven percent of couples' surveys said they got the support they wanted. They said they were given the tools their therapist needed to make more rational decisions about their relationships. The overall mental and physical health, as well as job results, improved as a side effect.

It Does not Take Much Time

Normally, a couple of therapists has seen and heard all of it, from the smallest issues to the most serious relationship problems. If couples are having joint meetings, it can take a few meetings to address the issues because therapists have various approaches and strategies. This could take more time to try and fix issues yourself and seeing a licensed professional would save you both time and energy.

You'll Know the Answers

Occasionally, counseling will convince you that you really are meant to be with your partner. Sometimes, it could demonstrate that your relationship isn't what any of you wants, which sometimes leads to divorce and separation. Regardless, couple counseling leads to questions answered, fewer "what-ifs," and more satisfaction.

CHAPTER 3

IRRATIONAL BEHAVIORS IN RELATIONSHIP

In this chapter, you will learn about the irrational behaviors that come with anxiety, negativity, and jealousy are discussed briefly and their identification and what to do instead of going after those irrational

behaviors.

A Misunderstanding of Emotions

The concept that women are irrational is always paired with a presumption that logical reasoning is superior to emotion, that rationality contributes to positive choices, and that emotions lead to weak ones. It couldn't be farther from the truth; evidence has demonstrated that it's not just that individuals are not emotionally involved that they don't make smart choices; people can't make decisions without emotions at all. While for effective action, emotions are important.

Philosopher Martha Nussbaum has written of emotions as a means of critical thought, evaluations of the present condition of one's life in the context of one's goals. In this way, optimistic feelings inform us that things are going better for us, and negative emotions inform us that something is wrong in our lives. This awareness provides a critical reference to a successful way of living.

That compares with a traditional perception of emotions as chaotic, stressful, and disruptive; they should be kept under control as such. With this mindset, often individuals lack the desire to analyze their own or other emotions and therefore have little awareness about their own or other emotional processes. Our society especially deprives men of opportunities for emotional expressiveness and understanding.

The word "irrational" is a refusal to acknowledge the reality of another.

Normally, in a case where the individual does not grasp whether this strong emotion is acceptable, what people mean by "irrational" behavior is a display of strong emotion. And just though the listener doesn't grasp the feeling doesn't mean it has no reasonable justification for this. Quite sometimes, the "irrational" word justifies and maintains cynicism because it implies the action is the product of such an intrinsically deficient or damaged individual that it defies and does not even deserve any fair person's consideration.

Romantic relationships are an arena in which emotions run wild, as do relational misunderstandings and subsequent irrationality allegations. Romantic relationships ask for intense feelings because they are attachment relationships. As adolescents, adults focus on comfort, security, and love dependent attachment relationships. Knowing the desires and vulnerability to one another moment to moment is the cornerstone to successful relationships. When one spouse feels endangered for relationship security (e.g., aggressive behavior or indifference), he or she will respond with strong emotion isolation, anger, sorrow, and disappointment, when experienced and voiced vigorously enough, such repeated responses may also appear irrational.

Emotional upheavals are wise indicators of one's course in life and the status of the most significant relationships. Invalidating another's reality by accusing him or her of being "irrational" leads to violating the person's right to self-determination. Buying into a description of oneself as "irrational" invalidates our own subjective reality and lacks the advantages that our emotions have as a guide to living a healthier life.

The Relationship Scorecard

What Is It?

The "keeping score" phenomenon occurs when someone you're dating goes on to accuse you of previous mistakes. When both partners do that in the relationship, it's what we consider the "relationship scorecard," where the relationship is a contest to see who gets the most messed up over the months or years, and therefore who is more indebted to the other.

You were a jerk at Cynthia's 28th birthday party back in 2010, and it's ruined your life ever since. Why? For what? What's next? So, there's not a week that goes by where you don't get reminded. But that's fine because the moment you catch your partner sending flirtatious text messages to a coworker cancels the ability to indulge in some productive jealousy, so it's sort of rational, right? Wrong.

Why Is It Toxic?

The Relationship Scorecard is a draining double-whammy. You're not just focusing on past failures to escape the current issue, but you're accumulating past guilt and resentment to manipulate your spouse into feeling guilty now.

If this continues on long enough, both sides will ultimately spend more of their energy seeking to show that they are less responsible than the other, rather than solving what created the present issue. Individuals waste their entire time trying to be less incorrect with each other than being more accurate with each other.

What to Do Instead?

Deal with problems individually, unless they are legitimately associated. It's obviously a recurrent concern anytime someone cheats habitually. Yet the reality that she embarrassed you in 2010 has nothing to do with each other, so don't bring it up.

It's crucial to remember that by deciding to be with your significant other, you choose to connect around all of their previous actions and behavior. In the end, if you do not embrace those, you do not accept your partner when you were troubled with things a year ago because you should have dealt with them at that time.

Dropping *Hints* and Other Passive Aggressions

What Is It?

Instead of expressing it directly and clearly, a companion attempts to nudge the other person in the right direction to sort it out. You'll find petty and subtle reasons to piss off your partner instead of revealing what really upsets you, so you'll feel entitled to complain to them.

Why Is It Toxic?

As it demonstrates, the two don't openly and clearly communicate. An individual has no excuse to be passive-aggressive if they feel free to express frustration or vulnerability inside a relationship. An individual would never feel the need to drop "hints" if they think they are not being judged or blamed for their honesty.

What to Do Instead?

State your thoughts and desires freely. So, make it clear that the other person is not necessarily responsible or entitled to certain emotions so that you would prefer to be helped by them. When they love you, they will be able to give this support almost always.

Holding the Relationship Hostage

What Is It?

If one person has a specific complaint or concern, he blackmails the other individual by challenging the entire commitment to a relationship. Of starters, if someone feels like you've been cold to them, instead of saying, "I feel like you're cold sometimes," they'll say, "I can't really date somebody who's cold to me."

Why Is It Toxic?

Keeping the relationship hostage is emotional blackmail and causes a lot of unnecessary tension. Even the smallest hiccup in the course of the relationship contributes to a potential commitment crisis. It is crucial for both people in a relationship to realize that unpleasant thoughts and feelings can be shared comfortably without it affecting the whole future of the relationship. Without the freedom to be honest, a couple will distort their own thoughts and emotions, contributing to an environment of distrust and exploitation developing.

What to Do Instead?

Getting upset or not liking something in your relationship is okay; that's called being a normal human being. Yet acknowledge that belonging to an individual is not the same thing as always loving an individual. You can be true to anyone, just not like them all. You may be eternally loyal to others, and often they may actually bother or harm you. In the alternative, two partners who can share advice and feedback without judgment or pressure will affirm their long-term devotion to one another.

Blaming Your Partner for Your Own Emotions
What Is It?

Imagine you're experiencing a rough day, and your companion isn't too compassionate or supportive about it—maybe they've been on the phone all day with other friends out of town, or they've been busy when you've hugged them. You decide to stay at home together and just watch a movie tonight, but your companion is hoping to go out to meet friends.

When your annoyance with your day – and your partner's reaction to it – comes up, you'll catch yourself lashing out because you're too mean and callous towards you. Of course, you have never asked for moral support, and your companion will naturally know how to make you feel better. They should have gotten off the line based on your crappy emotional condition to ditch their plans.

Why Is It Toxic?

Blaming our partners for our feelings is selfish and a perfect illustration of upholding improperly defined personal boundaries. This will quickly escalate to a co-dependent relationship if you create a trend in which your spouse is still liable for how you feel (and vice versa). It all needs to be planned- just to read a novel or watching television. When someone begins to feel frustrated, your personal concerns go out of the window, and you need to help each other feel comfortable then.

The main problem with the co-dependent traits is that they generate resentment. It is normal because, once in a while, one person gets angry at the other because he/she has had a bad day and is frustrated and needs attention. Even if it's an illusion that one partner's life should still revolve around the other's emotional well-being, it easily becomes very cynical and often manipulative about the partner's emotions and wishes.

What to Do Instead?

Take responsibility for your own feelings, emotions, and expect your spouse will take responsibility for theirs in exchange. There is a small but important gap between your partner being supportive and your partner is committed. It is to make certain sacrifices by intention and not because this is what is required. As long as all people in a relationship become accountable for each other's moods and downswings, it offers them both an opportunity to mask their real emotions and manipulate each other.

Displays of *Loving* Jealousy

What Is It?

Get pissed off anytime your spouse speaks, hugs, calls, emails, hangs out, or sneezes in the general proximity of another person, and then you carry out your anger on your spouse and try to control their behavior. That often contributes to insane things such as breaking into the email account of the partner, reading their text messages while they are in the shower, or sometimes following them across the town and showing up unannounced.

Why Is It Toxic?

Surprisingly certain people view this as a kind of love display, thinking, incorrectly, that if their mate isn't jealous that maybe they don't love them enough.

That is totally insane bullshit. In reality, it is all deceptive and controlling rather than being loving enough. And it creates needless stress and conflict by conveying a message of a loss of trust in the other. Worse yet, it's demeaning. If a woman is reluctant to allow her spouse to be alone with other attractive women, it implies she believes that he is either a) a liar or b) unable to regulate the impulses of the wife. That is a woman a person doesn't want to be with.

What to Do Instead?

Completely confide in your partner. It is a radical notion, but it is normal to have any jealousy. Yet extreme jealousy and behavioral control are indicators of your own feelings of unworthiness, so you will learn to cope with them and not impose them on others close to you. You're just going to push your companion away without resolving your jealousy.

Buying the Solutions to Relationship Problems

What Is It?

If there's a huge problem or concern in a relationship, you're covering it up with the anticipation and positive emotions that come with getting something great or going on a trip somewhere rather than fixing it.

For sure, a couple was experts at this one. And that never took them far: a big fat divorce and 15 years of barely talking to each other ever since. Afterward, they also claimed independently that the biggest challenge with their union had been to cover up their real problems with material gratification repeatedly.

Why Is It Toxic?

Buying things not only brushes the underlying problem under the rug (where it can always reemerge or worst the next time), but it still establishes a dangerous trend in the relationship. This is not a gender-specific problem but would use the "traditional" gendered scenario as an illustration. Imagine that if a woman gets angry with her husband/boyfriend by purchasing a present for the woman or taking her to a nice restaurant, the man "solves" the issue. It not only offers the woman tacit inspiration to find more ways to get upset with the man, but it also provides the guy absolute zero incentive to accept complete accountability for the relationship issues. Is that the end of it all? A husband who behaves like an ATM and a wife who is an unceasingly cynical and unheard-of woman.

What to Do Instead?

Tackle with the problem. Will it ruin the trust? Think of what it takes to restore. Does anybody feel disregarded or not appreciated? Speak regarding how to develop an appreciation for those feelings. Communicate!

There is nothing wrong with doing nice things for your partner after a fight to show support, regret, or reaffirm the bond. Yet, one should never use gifts or costly things to avoid dealing with underlying emotional issues. Gifts and vacations are called luxuries for a justification-you can really enjoy them when everything else is already great. If you try to manipulate these incentives to cover up your problems, you'll find yourself with a much bigger issue down the line.

Irrational Jealousy

Every single emotion is natural. The emotion isn't itself unreasonable. But how we make choices depending on our feelings may be unreasonable and affect negative behavior. Although many actions linked to emotions can trigger difficulties, emotions can be justified. Emotions seek to give us knowledge. When we get the details, we will then opt to take reasonable action. Emotions may, therefore, be mistaken like any details. Whether we make awareness of the emotion can't necessarily take to the precise nature of emotion.

Hence, our actions cannot resolve the difficulty given to our attention by the emotion or might even generate unnecessary difficulties. For starters, let's look at the feeling of agitation. Imagine a situation where an individual who has not been invited to a wedding is exempt from a particular event. In that situation, it would be normal for the individual to get hurt and upset. "Why does she not invite me? I have always been there for her." The angerproviding information then is that the person feels rejected and left out of a significant event. If the individual acknowledges this information, he may decide to respond by confronting his friend and voicing how he feels: "I don't understand why I wasn't included." In this case, he would figure out whether the slight was unintentional or whether there was a reasonable reason, or maybe his friend has an issue with him because she didn't deal with it. This allows him the opportunity to cope with the situation irrespective of what the problem is and to seek and fix it. What if, however, he misinterprets the anger: "She's always cutting me out. She doesn't really care about me," and in turn, he's assured of rejecting her. Even if, right before her wedding, he decides to write a harsh letter about how ungrateful and inconsiderate she is and give it to her?

The first reaction to the outrage was based on a reasonable and objectively reflective interpretation of the rage. Nonetheless, the second explanation was an erroneous definition that can inflict damage to the relationship beyond restoration. If it gets unreasonable, the emotion of jealousy is represented. Other definitions of the emotion of jealousy may be explored more and how to determine what the sensation entails. Finally, as it is unreasonable, the origins of excessive jealousy should be investigated, and opportunities to know how to handle jealousy should be concentrated.

What Is Jealousy?

Jealousy has long been seen as an obsession and ravaged society. Looking at classic literature or even the Bible, you'll find endless stories of jealousy and revenge. Throughout the early 1900s, researchers had researched jealousy among college students. One reviewer of this research says, "Jealousy is a fundamental instinct that bears a close resemblance to anger, terror, and sorrow, and demonstrates a correlation to the proprietary instinct. It is a defense against social instinct, and reciprocal help provides a clear antidote to jealousy (Withy, 1907); that is, jealousy is a specific instinct linked to the desire to control, particularly in relationships, and that the more people try to help one another rather than compete, the less jealousy is experienced. Jealousy is a loss-based emotion or fear of loss like a relationship or friendship. Other emotions are usually present, such as fear, rage, sorrow, or sadness. The person also experiences negative feelings of fear and thoughts. While Jealousy and Envy are somewhat similar, they are not considered the same emotion. Jealousy refers to the lack of something that the person already has, while envy is the longing for something that the person doesn't have. However, it can be argued that jealousy and envy can be nearly identical in certain circumstances. For example, if a person has been passed over for promotion, she may feel envious of the co-worker who has earned the promotion. Since she had not lost everything she had already (her job), it would not be called jealousy. We may, however, claim that she has lost something in her hands, such as her sense of adequacy or competence reflected by the promotion. In this case, it may be called jealousy to feel towards the co-worker; hence, while scientific research shows a clear difference between jealousy and envy.

When Is Jealousy a Normal Emotion?

As stated earlier, all of the emotions are natural. Jealousy is even more than a human instinct. Imagine a wife only discovering that her husband is about to leave her to another woman. Of which she would be jealous. In this case, the resentment that she experiences is part of her grief process. Her anger and jealousy are directed against her husband's focus of attention.

And many teenage girls, for example, encounter intense emotions in their friendships, such that if a friend decides to spend more time with another friend, they may feel rejection, frustration, and jealousy. Sadly, if, owing to anger and jealousy, they do not have assistance in establishing methods of solving this problem, they are likely to permanently break the bond. However, this increasing resentment is also a valuable lesson in learning how to build emotionally mature relationships. Ultimately, most teenagers understand that the case is not actually a failure and that their friendship hasn't been compromised. We realize there's more than one close friend that a particular individual may have. However, many individuals will not know this lesson, so, therefore, they begin to develop emotionally unstable relationships throughout adult life.

As you can tell from these cases, the general characteristic of natural jealousy is that it diminishes in intensity over time and only persists for a brief period of time. This is valid for most human feelings. Now, the time span may certainly differ depending on the circumstances, but the person will eventually resolve the emotion and move on psychically. Nonetheless, for unreasonable jealousy, the individual can stay stuck in the emotional experience for an indeterminate amount of time. But it can never improve without major reform initiatives.

What Is the Purpose of Normal Jealousy?

Motivation to Improve

Like every emotion, natural jealousy asks one to take a deeper look at a certain situation or ourselves. This will make us become more mindful of our own vulnerability so that we can overcome this.

Motivation to Resolve a Problem

And it could warn us that someone treats us in a hurtful way. For starters, each time a woman is out with her husband, he checks out other women and flirts with them. The woman may feel that other women are jealous of her. Yet if she examines the situation, she may be swayed by the jealousy that she's upset that her husband doesn't want to pay attention to her and that he doesn't care about her feelings. This acknowledgment allows her the chance to speak to him about her feelings and eventually fix the issue.

A Warning

Another jealousy purpose might be to warn us of some potential loss. Social connections had to be established throughout human culture in order to thrive. This makes sense in this context for people to foster jealousy as a means of motivating them to defend their resources to increase their likelihood of survival. Jealousy might not be as important for survival as other evolutionary behaviors, but within our social communities, it is still a vibrant force.

When we look at the previous case again, the woman's jealousy may have tried to express the possibility of her spouse abandoning her in terms of warning. However, we need to be careful about this concept because it may quickly trigger unreasonable jealousy without adequate proof. And it might be prudent for her to check her feelings with him, "I'm afraid you may abandon me when you pay so much attention to other women." His response might offer her an indication of this emotional warning's accuracy.

What Is Irrational Jealousy?

Irrational jealousy, also known as morbid jealousy in psychiatric literature, happens when the jealousy is not founded on reality or where the individual's jealousy appears out of proportion to the situation. Yet the feeling is more than just a flickering one. Usually, the individual not only dwells on jealousy but also participates in some form of negative behavior.

For example, a man who believes his wife is flirting with any man she talks to when she's only engaged in normal conversation may feel irrational jealousy. He not only constantly asks about her interactions or obsesses over her but often endlessly questions her about every aspect of her day. For the first time, she will console him and decides not to talk to other men, but she learns slowly that there is no reassurance that will fix the circumstance. She's going to become upset and resentful, which might cause what he's scared of —she'll be leaving him.

Another example (although that is more about envy) is someone who focuses obsessively on her neighbors' life and unfairly compares with her neighbor. However, she may also see the neighbor as undeserving of her good fortune and engage in vicious chatter with other neighbors that is a kind of revenge, the action often associated with jealousy or envy.

What Are the Problematic Behaviors That Occur with Irrational Jealousy?

Violence

The conduct that is of great concern is the tendency to perpetrate aggressiveness. It has been commonly reported to have been due to jealousy with the abuse of women. Nevertheless, having clear scientific evidence of the mechanism of rivalry and violence was challenging.

DeSteno et al. (2006) showed that jealousy causes aggression. Seeing that it is difficult to actually generate jealousy and violent acts in the research setting, not much research has been conducted to find out how jealousy leads to violent acts. Nevertheless, researchers DeSteno et al. (2006) have established a new method of using hot sauce as a retaliatory instrument and providing the spurned person the ability to impose vengeance on the other without having noticed anyone. As a consequence, they specifically found that the rejected individuals were more likely to attack the person who rejected them.

Researchers have noticed the violence to be focused on a reduction in selfesteem that culminated in heightened jealousy. In other terms, it will be noted that many that have not experienced a decline in self-esteem are unlikely to aggress, nor are those who have experienced a decline in self-esteem and no jealous feelings.

Stalking

Stalking is related to the issue of violence, which is an effort to intimidate someone, either by trying to convince the other of his / her loyalty or by more transparent forms of influence. The need for dominance is a core feature of stalking behavior. In fact, the individual may encounter a pattern of emotional connection, with feelings of frustration and jealousy.

Retribution

Another kind of aggression is revenge towards another person. Retribution, though, may not have to be outright aggression; in the context of gossip, it will be more subtle, passive-aggression behavior. In fact, revenge has become too easy these days across social networking sites as individuals are free to make hurtful remarks about someone who, in previous decades, may have been more private. Retribution often winds up escalating conflicts rather than fixing them. Imagine a situation in which a spouse is irrationally jealous of his wife, has access to their Facebook account, and under her name, makes nasty comments regarding her male friends.

Obsessive Talking or Questioning

A very common jealousy-related behavior is to continuously think about the issue of jealousy or to vigorously question people to determine if their irrational beliefs are correct. The problem with this interrogation is that there is no way to ensure whether it has not occurred. The questioning instead just persists, as the person is never assured.

Distrust

Another outcome of jealousy is distrust, which is an unpleasant situation and not conducive to the development of good relationship growth.

Causes of Irrational Jealousy

Fear of Loss

The most noteworthy characteristic of irrational jealousy is the fear of loss. This loss may take many types but generally falls into the definitions of lack of control, loss of self-worth, or loss of self-sense. An individual who perceives his opponent as having greater financial power may be a lack control. Ted Turner reported years ago that even the top multibillionaires were hesitant to make big charitable contributions because they were afraid of losing their spot among the wealthiest in the world. He said each of them continues to pay the same amount so that their standing stays the same. Which means they are going to be philanthropists and carry out benevolent acts without sacrificing their power.

And maybe they saw their position as an indication of self-worth in the documents, which is another type of failure that people fear. And lastly, the third type of failure is self-sense. An example of this could be a man who sees himself as the protector of his family and is terrified of sacrificing his wife and kids.

Inadequacy

Individuals who feel inferior to someone else or some particular ideals are more likely than others to experience jealousy or envy. Researchers at Northeastern University found that undermined self-esteem is a central contributor to irrational jealousy (DeSteno et al., 2006). Individuals whose self-esteem is based on an external source such as a relationship might be more susceptible to irrational jealousy as protecting existing sources of selfesteem becomes more difficult. At the same time, those who concentrate on love and self-acceptance of self-esteem are less prone to loss of self-esteem and thus less susceptible to jealousy.

Fear of Feeling

Although none of us like uncomfortable feelings, many people with extreme jealousy are especially terrified of feeling rejected or frustrated and are taking dramatic measures to try to avoid these feelings. Sadly, their aggressive behavior can create what they want to avoid, as well. Emotional anxiety or sensitization may arise from past experiences such as childhood rejection or a former partner that betrayed them.

Delusions

The origin could be based on paranoia in a limited group of individuals with jealousy issues. As such, this implies that the individual can experience a severe psychological disorder such as paranoid schizophrenia. One crucial path to discerning the difference between irrational jealousy and paranoia is for the deluded person to truly accept the truth of the faith. Although an adult with irrational jealousy is more likely to say, "I know I'm wrong, and it creates issues, but I can't help myself—this is how I feel."

Obsessions

Obsessions or, even more probable, Obsessive-compulsive Personality Disorder (OCPD) can be the cause of repeated behaviors in a particular group of individuals. The aforementioned causes of jealousy, such as fear of losing, inadequacy, and fear of feeling, can be reflected in these individuals, but they are bundled in a web of obsessions. Such people, often identified with reality, may have what is known as "overvalued ideation," which means that they might have enhanced difficulty in recognizing the irrationality of their jealous thoughts.

What Can Be Done Regarding Irrational Jealousy?

The method to deal with irrational jealousy depends upon the root cause.

Mental Illness

If the jealousy is psychotic, treating the delusions requires professional assistance and care. Individuals with OCD or OCPD require CognitiveBehavioral Therapy (CBT), at least, and can even benefit from medication.

Inadequacy

The individual has to address self-esteem issues for inadequacy problems. For certain individuals, this is fairly easy because they recognize low selfesteem. In this scenario, utilizing cognitive-behavioral development techniques to question unreasonable thinking may be helpful. For others, that may be more difficult as they do not realize the problems of self-esteem and may be dependent on feeling positive. They might need to do more research to gain a better perspective.

Fear of Feeling

People who are taking dramatic measures to avoid feeling miserable will know how to deal with their sorrow. In battling the excessive fear of feelings, we can recover from both grief counseling and CBT. It is likely that they already had previous unresolved grieving instances.

To begin with, a woman may have had a former unfaithful spouse and now has intense jealousy towards her present spouse, even if he has offered her no reason to be jealous. She was unable to cope adequately with her previous grief, and it is mirrored in her current relationship's jealousy.

Fear of Loss

The fear of losing the problem is handled in a manner that is close to the fear of feeling. The main difference is that the feeling of failure is geared into the future, as though the person were grieving something that has not yet happened. This may even find its roots in previous experiences of grief. So, the irrational assumptions are to be overcome and understand how to deal with sorrow.

Sometimes, when you meet someone that responds or behaves very often with a sequence of mere toxic characteristics. So poisonous, you have to be very cautious around them, and they don't strike towards you. They do this for the reason that they are not stable emotionally.

Victims of Irrational Jealousy

Several victims either lived or are in a relationship with a psychologically ill adult. These are some of the bad words they used to describe who these toxic individuals were: angry, violent, messy, clingy, whining, irritating, intimidating, offensive, inhuman, dangerous, deceptive, unreasonable, humiliating, difficult, demeaning, futile, destructive, sad, disturbed, disorganized, disturbing, dramatic, chaotic, painful, envious.

While the previous list of words is not a tool for diagnosis and cannot be applied in that manner, it gives us an insight into individuals that have gone through what life is like and what they are seeing as emotionally distressed adults. One term or one event does not render a bad personality—everyone has a bad day—if the individual shows a significant amount of actions exhibited in this category on a daily basis, we are seeing someone who is not emotionally stable, and they needed treatment.

Clearly, nobody has all the characteristics. Yet, not a lot of people have come across dealing with someone who frequently reveals a variety of things to be jaw-dropping. Working around anyone like that is "a living nightmare," in the words of some victim. What the perpetrators have depicted becomes an environment where things are routine for one minute, and a violent attack happens for the next. All is perfect for a minute until the moment further, with the smallest warning, there's a verbal assault that can last for a long time and leave you terrified, angry, disillusioned, and question your own rationality. These individuals are volatile in how they communicate with others, so you do not believe you can trust them—chaos always seems to be right near the edge, a small mistake or away from a misspoken word. You might have to move with caution for survival, even though on eggshells.

People remain in such relationships out of passion, concern, or desire, thinking their new precious gift or kindness act gets things better. This does not. No number of kindness or contrite would ever allow them to adapt.

The person compelled to change becomes the victim, which will have to acknowledge to either "bear it," as suggested by one survivor, or become so hesitant that with this emotionally unstable attitude, they cannot articulate their minds or consider living in the same environment. How people stay in these kinds of relationships is still confusing or a total secret, but one thing is for sure: the dysfunctional person needed help. So, you just can't personally repair them.

The last option you can try is to strive to obtain some professional assistance for them, but it may backfire. The psychologically ill sometimes cannot see something bad with them; they dismiss their work or say that you are a perpetrator, not them, and so they strike at you. But they need help. Professional help through somebody who is worthy of dealing with such individuals. You might also require a competent clinician to help you know that you have no liability for all like this.

When you encounter or are in a relationship with anyone like this, be vigilant not to get traumatized. When a crime happens, as is always the case, you will find support.

Besides the above words of the victims, the following can refer to the mentally disturbed individual:

- The intense show of frustration is somewhat out of proportion to the event or the situation.

- You became less contented, less hopeful, or less self-confident after you learn or have entered into a relationship with that person.
- The relation is best defined as "roller coaster" lows and highs.
- He is incapable of recognizing the implications of his derogatory remarks or acts and how they will affect others, also including relatives or community.
- Behave in circumstances that are often unacceptable or absurd. Every time, it appears to fall apart or get mad at the slightest tension.
- Arguments of few seconds will continue for days or hours without any effort to change or interrupt them.
- The smallest incident will lead her/him to get angry and act out.
- Cases of brawls, fights, or direct confrontations are common. Sometimes for total strangers or even medical providers such as a therapist, verbal altercations or disputes appear to be a part of life.
- You can't seem to be comfortable, calm, or "holding down" with this person.

- Those who are close will "check" periodically to see what the current "mood" is.
- It is defined by some as "unstable" or called for throwing away things or destroying property.
  - Says that they forgive, but they never do: mistakes, injustices, or failure are specifically remembered for usage in upcoming arguments.
  - One has got a "short temper" and a low degree of frustration. Incapable of sincere empathy, sympathy, or love yet even requiring you or anyone to do so.
  - You often feel afraid to speak or respond from fear of the potential reactions that this person might have towards you or that they might injure themselves.
  - You feel trapped by the person in certain aspects.
  - Using guilt as a retaliation tactic or puts you down to boost their self-worth.
  - They also cry out not just with remorse but also with vengeance. Even appallingly.

And if any of the above words align with you, they can be a person with emotional instability. Although these entities will seek to make it look like that everything is at fault because of you or that you don't have any sense, that's because they're bad at fault. There might be several bases as to why they are so, but in no way does that justify how they make you feel or treat you. You do need professional care, and it isn't your duty to become the human punching bag of the mentally distressed individual.

Your duty is to separate yourself and your children, if there is need to be, from this sort of character before they give you any harm. Regardless of what people might suggest about you, remind yourself this: "You never have a social obligation to be marginalized." We've all had anyone tell us anything that appears to be completely off the wall and tried to argue with them—trying to convince them to see it our way. Will it work so much like that? The quick answer to this is Never. Never have.

Then, the argument tends to intensify out of control with neither of you responding to the other, and it's usually getting nasty.

When people get upset, the rational mind goes off, and the animal mind takes over. They begin to respond out of panic, triggering their response to fightor-flight stress responses. And it's like attempting to explain something about someone that speaks a separate language than you, seeking to argue for someone who has separated themselves from their rational brain.

So, when someone around us begins responding to us from the place of fear, from the wounded ego, this causes our own responses to fear as well. When that occurs, the sides struggle to respond or negotiate rationally, and the relationship becomes an unreasonable and unproductive thing.

So, What's the Alternative?

The alternative is to make your own reaction conscious. Your original thoughts can sound insane like this. That's just not true. That is not real. It is out of the wall. They are imprecise.

In reality, the first goal is to be respectful of these emotions, take a deep breath, and remember that you can't change someone else's beliefs. You don't have much influence over what they're doing, how they're behaving, or whether they're treating you or themselves.

The toughest part of this process is recognizing the insufficient control over others. If you tolerate the failed effort to connect with them in that case, you may opt to take an approach that would help you: either comfort them because they are responsive to you or walk away and take control of your own feelings.

It can be incredibly difficult. We desire too desperately to convince people to see "the truth," particularly those we care for.

We want them to avoid being crazy and reconcile with us. It's scary when the people we worry about quite making sense.

That is why the best way to feel safe is not to slip into the chaos. We give in to the crazy as we try to scream, defend, clarify, yell, etc.

Someone is not present much of the time in an emotionally driven setting or is vulnerable to warmth. When you know that this entity is inaccessible to you in this situation from prior experience, so the only safe and rational choice is to get out of the situation—not with anger or remorse, but with solid, gentle detachment.

It usually takes about 30 minutes for a human's higher brain to come online while stressed and irritated but wait at least half an hour before seeking to reengage. You will always search for opportunities to see how the other person is doing.

If they start to settle down, maybe you should speak to them about the situation that prompted them to respond from a wounded position. But it could be easier to just let it go. Experience will show you which benefit is greatest.

It takes bravery not to jump in to try to reassure the other individual to quit "acting nuts." Some of us care too much for preventing the feeling of helplessness over others that we will do almost anything not to accept the reality.

After being disengaged, humbly welcome the feeling of helplessness and let the feeling float into you. It's for sure that you will be empowered because you're able to take proper care of yourself, rather than arguing for someone who can't listen to you or acknowledge you.

CHAPTER 4

SPECIFIC PROBLEMATIC AREAS FOR COUPLES

This chapter covers all the problematic areas intruding on couples' or partners' life in detail. What can be chronic or unproductive arguments and how they can be ignored are also mentioned in detail.

Some people naturally act negatively, which affects everyone and every situation they're a part of. Other people are having a bad day, moment, or going through a bad time in their lives. They don't know how to handle this situation, so they react negatively.

Once you realize that you have nothing to do with their negative reaction, it's easier to take a step back and analyze the situation accordingly. Sure, you might decide to give the person what they want but then explain to them this is the only time and let go of the black cloud they tried to place above you once they leave.

Another way to handle people who are acting negatively is to do your best to smile and bring peace to the situation. You might find this is easier to do than other times, and this is fine. During the times you can't smile, do your best not to react without reflecting on your emotions and taking time to count to ten or focus on a few deep breaths. In a sense, you want to become the bigger person in the situation by doing everything you can to remain calm before you react. Of course, you can also choose not to say anything, which is sometimes best if you know that you can't keep the peace if you speak.

One way to help you keep the peace is to remember not to judge their behavior. You might judge someone because they don't perform like someone else or yourself.

It's easy for you to think if you can do something, then someone else can do it. For example, if you can bite your tongue, so you don't talk out of turn, everyone else should do this as well, right? Wrong. There are many reasons why some people struggle to understand when they are speaking disrespectfully. It can stem from their childhood, or they are unhappy with their lives and taking their anger and sadness out on other people.

When you start to feel yourself becoming more frustrated with the person's negative behavior, you have a couple of options to take. First, you can try to talk to them about their negativity. Depending on your relationship with the person, this might be next to impossible and cause the situation to become worse. Before you even consider this option, there are a lot of factors to weigh in on. First, you need to analyze the person's behavior. Try to understand why they are negative and note if there is a way you can help ease their emotional and mental pain. Second, you need to analyze what they're saying. For example, do they complain about one person often, or are they stressed about life events? By understanding the person's behavior, you can get an idea of why they react negatively and use this information when talking to them.

If you decide to talk to the person, make sure you do so in a very calm and compassionate way. You don't want to make the situation worse by making them feel like you're attacking their behavior, so do your best to ensure they understand you're trying to help them so you can assist in the problem they brought to your attention. Unless you have a close bond with the person, telling them that you're struggling with their negative behavior will make them feel like you're attacking them. Most people act negatively because they have a problem they don't know how to fix. Think of their negativity as a way of reaching out for help.

If you really have trouble tolerating the negativity the person brings but you're not comfortable talking to them, do your best to keep your distance. If they come into your office to talk, assess the situation to see if they need someone to talk to, vent to, or if they just want to be negative. If you don't like the answer you give yourself, try to find a way to talk about something more positive, explain that you're working on a project you need to get done or ask if they would like to talk later. While you can't avoid your coworkers forever, you can prepare yourself to deal with the negativity by asking to talk at a later time so you can get your work completed on time.

Negative Coworkers

Negative coworkers are one of the most significant problems for people. It's easy to make sure you're hanging out with positive people. You know who your positive friends are and the ones who tend to bring more negativity; it's easier to distance yourself from them. Even if you maintain contact, you can control the contact. You don't need to see them every day and can let their text or social media messages sit until you're prepared to help them or listen to their negativity. However, when it comes to coworkers, it's harder to distance yourself. You see them a few times during the week and usually for several hours at a time.

You need to listen to their negative thoughts during meetings, lunch, and throughout the day—especially when they corner you in your office and start talking.

The negative energy that your coworker brings to you can stay with you on your way home. You might not realize it, but you can bring home other people's negative energy, which can cause you and your family to become more negative. Other than cleansing your mind with meditation and keeping your home as peaceful as possible, you'll need to find other ways to work with your coworker but not let their negative energy consume your life.

You already have some tips in your mind that will help you, such as knowing that you can't control their behavior. Other tips already discussed are to not take anything personally and analyze the situation or behavior. Unfortunately, sometimes you need a few more tips to help you get through the day, so you don't become negative and begin overthinking everything.

Another way is to resist getting involved in office politics. You already know that politics are a touchy subject for everyone, and this can create a lot of tension. For example, your coworker comes up to you in the break room and starts talking about what another coworker said about your supervisor. The best course of action for you to take is to politely state, "I'm sorry, I try not to get involved in these types of topics." In a sense, you're politely telling your coworker that you don't want to get involved in the work gossip, no matter how interesting it is, because it leads to negative thinking and then overthinking.

When you set these types of limits, you're taking control of the environment around you. You can't control the whole office environment, but you can control your little space. You can control what you get involved with and how you handle situations that can cause you to overthink. If your coworker doesn't listen to what you have asked, then you need to do your best to keep your distance and limit contact as much as possible.

One key step to take when it comes to a negative coworker is to not give them sympathy. Even if they are gossiping about another coworker, watch everything you say and your tone when you respond because negative people crave sympathy and like to be the center of attention. Don't give them what they are trying to seek. The truth is, if the negative coworker doesn't get what they want from you, they will leave you alone and go to someone else.

Another way is to do your best not to bond with them. It's easy to want to bond with people who are negative when you first meet because you want to help them. You want to try to understand them so you can help them become more positive. This is the moment when you feel that you can try to change them, but you can't change them. The only way you can protect yourself from following negative thoughts is to resist trying to help change them, which means you don't form a connection. This doesn't mean that you don't communicate at all. It doesn't mean that you're not polite to them or you refuse to work with them. It simply means you have a working relationship with the person, and that's all it is. Keep the relationship as professional as possible.

Verbal Abuse

In a relationship, verbal abuse happens from nowhere. It becomes even more cynical and manipulative, leading people to doubt themselves on the receiving end, worrying whether they are overreacting or even blaming themselves. Typically, verbal harassment happens in private areas where no one else may interfere and gradually becomes a normal mode of contact within a relationship. To those who suffer it, verbal harassment is mostly marginalized, and it eats away at your self-esteem, finding it impossible to reach out to a mate.

Many people who witness it in their heads rationalize the violence and don't really know it's an inappropriate method of contact. But this doesn't make those on the receiving end any less distressing or emotionally taxing.

Basically, verbal violence is a tool in order to retain dominance and authority over someone. There are a number of various types that verbal violence can take, rendering it much more challenging to understand. Of starters, verbal harassment involves being exposed to name-calling on a daily basis, feeling continually demeaned or belittled, and being subjected to a partner's silent treatment.

When you can't say if your companion is "funny" or "belittling," here are a number of say-tale indications that your relationship is deteriorating.

10 Most Commonly Verbal Abuse Patterns

These are the 10 most commonly verbal abuse patterns to look out for in a relationship:

1. Name-Calling

This kind of verbal violence is perhaps the most readily identifiable. This involves being named names and/or getting yelled at constantly. Arguments that often turn to shouting in a debate and utilizing offensive words are both indicators that your relationship with your spouse is anything but safe. Partners back away from a dispute in a stable relationship or seek to talk about the problem. The offender can scream in a verbally abusive relationship unless they get what they want.

Example: "You fool, you have made me angry now!"

2. Condescension

Subtle sarcasm and a cynical tone of voice need not be a regular feature of companion relationships. It can also mean being the frequent object of laughs from the mate. It may start sweet, which is why it always goes undetected, but with time, condescension is abominable.

Example: "No wonder your weight is still complaining; look how clean your plate is!

3. Manipulation

Often detecting a manipulative personality can be simple, particularly when someone constantly forces their spouse to do something, they're not really happy with to do. By comparison, deception may be difficult to spot. It can be subtle, like flipping around circumstances and laying the blame on the person being victimized.

Example: "If you truly liked me, you wouldn't say that, or you wouldn't do that."

4. Criticism

It's ok to have positive criticism when questioned on occasion; it's good, to be frank with your mate. Nevertheless, persistent disappointment and belittling of a significant other is not good and may result in a substantial loss of self-esteem over time.

Example: "Why do you get so disorganized? I can count on you many times for destroying our nights out!

5. Demeaning Comments

This is dangerous if a companion puts you down using demeaning remarks relating to your race/ethnic heritage, class, faith, history, in general. This need not need to be systematic; if it occurs once, it will certainly happen again and would not be minimized. A companion that likes you and values you won't use something that's innate in you to bring you down.

Examples: "I'm not shocked, you're Asian, you're all doing that" or "you girls, weeping for nothing as useless cries."

6. Threats

While that may be an easy one to know, it's not always the case. Threats may be made up in a way that lets them sound as though they're "not that serious" or in a manner that makes you doubt whether you've heard it correct. Yet danger is a hazard, and they are not resorted to by a romantic friend to get their way.

Examples: "I'm going to injure myself if you're leaving me tonight" or "If you don't do this, you might notice your cat is outside spending the night!"

7. Blame

Blame is one of the most prevalent types of verbal violence, which entails continually imposing the blame on a spouse for one's behavior rather than accepting responsibility for them. These might involve punishing a person over events that they have nothing to do about, punishing the spouse for the actions of the victim.

Examples: "You are the cause we're never on schedule!" and "See what you've done to me now!"

8. Accusations

Repeated allegations sometimes arising from extreme envy are a type of verbal assault.

Being continually suspected of something also causes a person to start wondering whether they are doing anything wrong / inappropriately dressing/speaking too often, etc.

Examples: "I bet you are deceiving on me! "Or, "I noticed you flirting with your manager again when I was talking with your dull teammates."

9. Withholding

A spouse can often step away from a confrontation, choosing to allow the dust to settle and partake in a more meaningful discussion without flaring up emotions. While that is certainly a hallmark of a good relationship, the silent treatment, also called withholding, is not. Withholding can involve your companion failing to reply to your calls if they don't get what they want or avoiding you outright.

Example: You are debating choices for restaurants because you don't want to go for your partner's option. They're leaving the room and declining to speak to you because you're "bad."

10. Gaslighting

Gaslighting means discounting the desires of a person and having them question whether their thoughts are insignificant and/or fake. This is a very popular sort of emotional violence which, since it can be subtle, which highly coercive, sometimes goes undetected. Gaslighting will render you feel lonely and incapable of voicing your feelings. Gas-lighted individuals frequently catch themselves, sorry for actions they never performed.

Examples: "Why are you so focused on everything?

Separating Work from Home Life

A job-family dispute is not an individual occurrence but can influence everyone, including family members and coworkers/supervisors, around them. However, analysis has concentrated mainly on work-related effects— relationship dispute on an entity basis, rather than from a dyadic, social, or corporate level. There is increasing literature on the convergence burden of job-family disputes with others. The mechanisms by which these systems occur, and the long-term convergence tension effects for others, remain unknown, however. Researchers ought to raise deeper questions regarding how the role of parent's job-family tension impacts children over the span of life-from adolescence through adulthood. Scholars will need to discuss how one spouse's job-family dispute influences the everyday lives and emotional wellbeing of another.

Finally, organizational research will also challenge how work-family tension interactions influence person and group-level dynamics between coworkers. More generally, such kinds of research will help explain the wider effect of practice –family dispute on culture.

In the term work-family dispute, the concept of 'family' must be extended to encompass alternate social types and behaviors beyond the commonly established nuclear family. Job-family rivalry with small children is often synonymous with the conventional portrayal of the dual-career pair. Unmarried nonparents globally, however, often encounter work-family tension dependent on the responsibilities to those within one's social network, such as extended family members, friends, and neighbors. In fact, the concept of what constitutes family may incorporate alternate types of marriage, such as pairs of same sex with and without children. Job-family dispute analysis—including concepts and methodology of study—ought to develop to include such less prevalent interactions.

The Effect of Occupational Conditions

Evidence suggests that the work-family dispute relationship is influenced by working circumstances and the atmosphere of the workforce. Others claim that working environments will have a greater difference than the real number of hours employed. Particularly significant are flexibility and power over schedules and task material, which are not only correlated with employee fulfillment and occupational wellbeing but have also been shown to alleviate tension between work and family. For example, workplace autonomy was correlated with higher rates of work-family balance for both men and women.

Supportive bosses, exposure to insurance, and the opportunity to choose family-friendly choices are all critical in this matter, which may help parents properly handle conflicting jobs that the family demands. Often prevalent in the careers and corporate world, the organizational culture, which demands full time and energy commitment to the job, may be a serious obstacle to family life. Indeed, becoming productive implies staying childless for some people in the top positions, especially women.

On the other side, non-standard operating hours have proved to be counterproductive. Rotating and night shifts are correlated with greater marital dysfunction and tension between the working and home. Shift employment is often a source of tension for single moms, not just because of elevated rates of physical discomfort but also because these kinds of occupations make it tougher for them to find childcare, thus raising tension and parental responsibility for the wellbeing of their babies.

The downside among single parents often derives from the reality that they are far more inclined than most parents to job non-standard work hours. Since they are usually younger and less well-educated, single parents are more likely to focus in low-status job sectors with stressful and restrictive schedules, have less flexibility over the work cycle, and provide little advantages, if any. Single parents are also especially prone to extreme timesqueezes.

Sexual Issues and Problems

The fact is that, when it comes to sex, both men and women continue to talk about the same issues, particularly while they are in a long-term relationship. Below are eight of the most popular concerns generally receive from partners, along with tips for flipping upside down a partner's frown.

1. Laziness

When the spouse has started doing their sharing between the sheets, seek a discreet solution instead. Playfully lament how much you enjoy turning his or her signature in bed, be it a switch, twist, or move. A gentle note that tango needs two may be all it takes. When this doesn't fit, then opt for a straighter solution. Inform your companion politely that you found he or she is not displaying the same effort and inquire why. If there is no reason (and if you're confident there are no medical issues), be frank about how his or her lack of enthusiasm in bed sometimes takes the pleasure out of sex for you. When your partner is involved in your relationship, he or she steps up to the challenge with love. In the meantime, revising your own rambunctiousness may be a pleasant idea. A lazy companion, in or out of bed, isn't worth the effort.

2. Boredom

Can you schedule your watch when he is going to hand you over? See her touch fall a mile away? Long-term sex will gradually become easy to predict with the same individual. So, while there's something soothing about physical intimacy, if it's the only meal on the table, it may foster disdain. Experiment with different positions to get out of bedroom isolation, focus on improving your physical abilities, or shock your lover by asking them for an intimate vision or a filthy dream to kick-start your romantic imaginations. Change the way you treat yourself in bed. Normally, if you are silent, wake up the neighbors. If you happen to be loud, dial it down. Take the pace if you're usually sluggish and steady. Place a sex toy under the pillow of your spouse, whether it is a high-tech vibrator, a feather tickler, or a heating/cooling lubricant for extra vibration.

3. Ignoring the Connection Between Emotional Physical Intimacies

How a pair view each other outside the bedroom affects the quality of their love life strongly. Nasty, nagging, and disruptive spouses rarely enjoy the ultimate relationship. Strengthen the connection by improving contact, prioritizing a couple of times, letting your partner feel valued, and following the attitude of modesty, open-mindedness, and a team player. Replace the criticism or disdain with a polite, affectionate sound in your speech. Do the "small stuff" you think it will be making your companion get a happy day. It is your best bet for a hotter night.

4. Electronic Interlopers

Laptops, computers, I-Products, and smartphones provide a way to get into the bedroom and minimize private downtime for a couple. When you respond to a text or change your Facebook status instead of snuggling your sweetheart, you unwittingly send out the impression that your companion is not as fascinating or significant as the individual on the other side of whatever device is in your hand. Render your dormitory a technology-free space. Charge the kitchen counter on your mobile phone and drop your device in the living room. Reclaim your double suite.

5. A Negative Body Image

In long-term marriages, improvements in the body are expected. When there are females, they get pregnant and give birth. They are speeding up. They are adding weight and losing their eyes.

Health issues and everyday pressures are now taking a toll on the body. The health rates are increasing and falling down. Such shifts may cause people to become self-conscious about their bodies, causing them to cover up more and have a little intercourse. Couples should adopt a healthy lifestyle to improve their body image. As especially, they will tend to complement the beauty and desirability of each other. Beauty truly is in the beholder's eye.

6. Disparate Sex Drives

If you're the one with an inherently higher sex desire, don't annoy your mate, moan when you don't understand it, mock their lower desire or try to have sex somewhere. Act as an individual. If your drive is incredibly strong, the burden off your companion is lifted by some "alone time." Recognize that there is a link between physical and emotional affection, whether you are the one with the lower drive, and that the fair and caring demands for sex from your spouse are vital to your relationship as a happy, long-term couple. No magic number remains. The secret to this is harmony.

7. Missing the Connection Between Mental and Physical Arousal

Many guides on intimacy highlight the value of improved approaches, different poses, and sex toys, all items that help you feel stronger. That's awesome, but the calculation is just half that. Couples will always work on activating the strongest sex organ— the brain. Sex is at its strongest, while couples are switched on emotionally as well as physically. One of the writers blends the visual eroticism of the *50 Shades of Grey* genre with kinky "how to" sex tips in his new novel, 50 Ways to Play: BDSM for Decent People, which will help traditional lovers transform their dreams into actual play in the bedroom.

8. Exhaustion

True old-fashioned exhaustion is a key concern among the active couples in today's bedroom. Tackle the bedtime ritual as a team to overcome it. Ask what you should do to help cool down your companion without going out. You should finish the supper dishes, put the kids in bed, or allow the companion some space to complete his or her job papers. If you have identical habits, so you will go to bed at the same moment. It not only improves the odds of remaining together but also tells the spouse you are in it together.

Here are further 11 more interrupting issues regarding sex between couples and some of their compensations:

1. Female clients frequently claim they are too busy to be through intercourse at the time. It is especially true of many mothers because the parental strain will block some sexy thoughts. It might seem counterintuitive, but it will help to plan age. When you realize when it can happen, you may be more prepared to adapt to it. Alternatively, adding any excitement by sex instruments or different sex styles will serve to hold you alive and present.

2. That story of how unfeeling, sex-obsessed robots are doing a disservice for dudes. Men sometimes feel confused by the idea that they are sentimental Neanderthals. Some show that they really want to get better inside and outside the bed, but they really don't know-how. Make things easy for him by being open to a monkey see through your own emotions; the monkey does complex. When he feels mushy, you should still be super affectionate—it's just about constructive reinforcement.

3. If one individual feels the other doesn't have enough of the good times to go, anger will bubble up. Waiting for your mate to start and getting upset when it doesn't happen, then you should do something while you're in the mood. Stop selfishness from destroying your relationship. And if you're on the other end of the spectrum, realize that the appeal your companion makes for you to initiate intercourse more frequently is just about feeling wanted, and making that initiative will massively strengthen your relationship.

4. At happy hour, you may have noticed this one across the table because if it relates to you, you know how annoying it can be. When you're in the heat of the moment, it's better to literally remind your mate what's important for you by putting their hand in the right places. When you're going to talk out, it's good to phrase what you expect constructively. You appreciate it so much when the partner is doing XYZ because it sounds less of a suggestion and more of promoting what they're actually doing.

5. Luckily, this has a humorous remedy. Every day, you can tell each other one thing you admire about the other person. If that's too bad for your tastes, add the little gestures that you originally depended on to express intimacy when you first started dating: holding hands, throwing your arms around each other when seated together, touching each other's necks, etc.

6. Although it's cool if both parties are in it only for the physical release, if you want an emotional bond but don't sense it, things get more turbid. That is what "empty species," which doesn't sound very interesting. To further banish the sensation, function outside of the bedroom to encourage intimacy. Spend more time together, discover fresh, simple experiences that will help you build a connection, and seek different ways to offer joy to you and your companion.

7. When a straight pair attempts to conceive, the guy may feel like he is working on the order. When you're ovulating, there will be a compromise between articulating and spontaneity.

Communication is crucial to deciding whether to cross this boundary because certain male partners would want to learn every aspect of your period, and some would like to remain less sensitive to the details. And if the end objective is to reproduce, no matter when he falls, you also will put a sense of anticipation back into sex. Doing stuff like wearing lingerie and sending sexy messages will help make a baby seem enjoyable rather than a burden.

8. While the lack of sleep and tension will send serious walloping to the sex drive, it's not all gone. There are a number of people that, since beginning a family, we're willing to restore a satisfying dating existence. Find out whether logistical would deter you from feeling happy or whether the question is just physical in the first place. It also has something to do with unexpressed or unmet social communication and affection requirements. One way to access the real problem is to arrange an appointment with a psychiatrist who would be willing to speak to you all about it.

9. Feeling that your companion doesn't understand that you're destroying your link to each other, which

just makes the situation worse. There are couples discussing this clearly in counseling instead of dancing around the subject. Let's imagine an example: We need to say, 'I feel like Y when you do X,' because there's no space for confusion. Such declarations regarding" I "are important to making your spouse not feel threatened.

10. If there ever had been a moment to tread carefully, it should have been it. While premature ejaculation becomes a problem at the outset of the relationship—except with the very first potential nervousness—it happens as a whole problem. When you two have sex for the first time, an expert suggests that you hold your confusing emotions under control and pass them on, either to other activities, whether he's up for it or to anything non-sexual. When it occurs again, that is an issue that doesn't go anywhere. Gently persuade him to visit a specialist and make sure there is no underlying reason to get some guidance about what's going to help his body cope while it's raring to go.

11. Once the honeymoon period has faded off; this one also forces its way through the relationship. The person who desires more sex may feel neglected, but without a conversation, their spouse does not know it. Luckily, adjustments will save the day. Discuss how much you would like to be sexually involved together and hammer out a schedule in the middle ground. Set dates you've always decided to be romantic and make a running list of items you'd want to check out.

Experimenting with what's turning on will help you look forward to having good sex back.

In-Laws Controversies

At any point, most families are dealing with in-law problems. Of starters, you may feel that your in-laws don't support you or your partner is too dismissive of them. And they have an opinion on everything that goes from where you stay to how you raise your babies. Having problems with your in-laws doesn't mean that you are in an abusive relationship. It is similar to war. Conflicting doesn't ruin a relationship. Yet, they will do things poorly. So, the same is out with the in-law challenges. What counts is how such problems are treated. Here's how balanced couples treat their in-laws.

Healthy Couples Realize Their In-Laws Are Unique People

Healthy families are coping with their in-laws and understanding that they are special individuals in many respects. The families have a nature of their own. Healthy partners know that society is "not incorrect or evil, just special."

Healthy Couples Make an Effort Regarding Their In-Laws

They know the role their in-laws play in the life of their partner. They handle them politely. They join social functions. They "require their in-law's access to their families." In other words, they make an attempt, even if "they do not necessarily approve, appreciate the complexities, practices or customs of the families, or even look forward to the future together."

Healthy Couples Set Cool Boundaries with Their In-Laws

They should have frank discussions regarding their desires with their partners and build a roadmap on which all of them consent. For example, your partner is Cool with his mom coming by unannounced. You really don't. And you agree that you ought to contact family members beforehand and make sure it's a pleasant moment to come over.

Healthy Couples Distinct Their Own Relationship from Their In-Laws

And they are not contracted to them, no matter how confusing or unpleasant their in-laws can be. And when the in-laws are extremely challenging to contend with, happy people make a special attempt to be good to their spouse. They might say "I love you" or execute a nice gesture.

Healthy Couples Distinct Their Spouse from Their InLaws

For e.g., Mom might be invasive and dismissive of a man, but a happy couple knows that her conduct may not represent how the guy thinks regarding the stuff she reflects on.

Healthy Couples Keep Communicating

Term-processing is one of the most critical techniques a pair has to negotiate with in-laws. So, they are thinking about their own positions. They are attentive. They fully sympathize with the emotions of each other.

Healthy Couples Don't Take It Personally

A stable pair will understand and cope with the reality that their parents are human beings, with natural and complicated human emotions. They are seeking to learn where they come from, so they're empathizing.

Tips for Dealing with In-Laws

Here are further five suggestions for dealing with your in-laws:

Set Boundaries

Define the boundaries you want to establish for your in-laws. For example, if your mother-in-law is taking over your kitchen each time she comes, speak to your spouse about it. Then have a polite yet straightforward talk with her about the problem.

You might suggest the following: "Mother, we love that you do care and want to help us out by doing some cooking and know that you really enjoy it, but we would appreciate it if you let Mary (wife) take the lead in our kitchen. If you want to help, she would really appreciate it if you were willing to create the salad for dinner tonight."

Remember It's Only an Opinion

Remembering so much of what we are taught is an idea, not fact, helps. And if your mother-in-law recommends that you can feed your son with a different diet, note that you don't have to accept it, fight it out of existence or view it as a critique of you. Although we can't avoid talking to an in-law, we can regulate how we hear them.

Remember Your In-Laws Are People

They are like you, have desires, fears, suspicions, and emotions. Treat them not as guardians, just like all other individuals you slowly become acquainted with.

Respect Your Spouse's Attachments

It helps to consider the commitment of the husband to his kin as something to be valued. For starters, if the regular calls your husband makes to his father are valuable to him, it is therefore valuable for you to recognize and acknowledge that.

Take Deep Breaths

Take a pause to relax as you are about to hit a breaking point. Find a peaceful spot, like a bathroom or taking a stroll. When you relax, reflect on the good qualities of your in-laws—such as "they just enjoy our family"—and note that you can't influence or alter them.

Your in-laws are important to your family, and they're part of your life. It is up to you all to find a way to make your time as fun as possible with extended family.

CHAPTER 5

UNDERSTANDING EACH OTHER

This chapter highlights the importance of mutual understanding and all the other aspects that come along with it to understand one another. It is a crucial step towards building a healthy relationship. There is a fine distinction between understanding and being defensive. Understanding is where you want to learn and appreciate the reason behind their actions, and defending is where you start explaining all their acts only to comfort yourself.

Why Is Understanding Important in a Relationship?

Now, on to the issue, why is it important? Think about all sorts of relationships here (friends, families, marriage, professional, etc.). Just take an example:

- He: It's 12 o'clock she has to call me; it is my birthday.

- She: I'm not going to call him at 12, however, I will surprise him in the morning.

Here he got two options, either blame her for not calling at 12 o'clock or just have patience and wait to know the cause.

Another example is:

- She: He told me he'd never speak about his ex-wife or see her, so why the heck he'd seen her today.
- He: She may be my ex-wife, but she needed support today. I wish that "she" isn't angry at me.

Whether she should fight here, or she should actually want to understand his point of view.

So, why is understanding important in a relationship?

- Two-person can, at the same time, have a separate viewpoint on the same problem.
- The scenario might not be what you perceive appropriate. The individual can have several explanations for not reacting to you.
- Everyone deserves a shot.
- Every relationship relies on the perception of one another.

- Value someone else's opposing opinion.

To want and learn but not explain the purpose of the conduct. Knowing that another individual was correct to have a totally different viewpoint than ours.

- To realize that you will always respect each other without feeling the same way, without deciding on anything, and without simply obeying each other.

- Know when to say, "let it be."

In any relationship, the degree of understanding defines the strength of your relationship.

Everyone wants to be noticed, heard, and understood. We like that from our partners in particular. We want our spouse to tell, "Yeah, I listen. Yeah, I do. Yeah, I understand the pain that you have. I'm sorry that hurts, and here I am. We like our spouses to be involved in what is going on within our heads and to care about it.

The fundamental human desires are the need to be seen, heard, and recognized.

One of the most frequent concerns relationship therapists receive from their clients is that they don't get that from their spouses—even if it's strong and essential to healthy relations. "Feeling noticed, validated, and recognized contributes to greater trust and relational growth." When we don't have that, we feel excluded and like we don't matter, which may weaken our bond over time.

There is a common (inaccurate) assumption that our spouse's interpretation implies we have to agree with them. However, you might absolutely disagree with that. Rather understanding simply means listening thoroughly and intently to our spouses. It comes down to understanding what they claim. This involves asking your spouse, "I believe I understand you. So, let me check: What you're saying is, "That implies sticking through this process" because your companion doesn't need to explain their viewpoint even more since they realize you get it. You really understand it, even though you don't approve.

Below are the suggestions shared on how we can "get it" and better understand our partners.

Tips to Better Understand the Other Person

Be Fully Present

You do not need to do something while your spouse is talking. You don't have to try to fix that situation or make things smoother. "The only role is to have the partner express their human experience with another being."

Understand First

"Make sure to understand first, then be understood. Seek not to compose the responses while the partner is speaking. It also prevents you from digesting what they are saying thoroughly, which impedes genuine comprehension. "They would obviously reciprocate with interest regarding what you think and experience as your spouse feels heard so you will have a chance to express your viewpoint."

Avoid Complaints and Defensiveness

Defensiveness and complaints are characteristics of dysfunctional interactions that keep you from really intimately bonding. When someone criticizes and argues, they put their partner unintentionally on the defensive. It shows your spouse that "it's not me; it's you." "And the key is to accept any accountability, just a little iota, a weensy tidbit—"I've understood your point, I've agreed I'd... I've got to..." It's always good to inform your spouse how you feel about what you need.

Manage Your Own Stuff

It is important to remember that knowing our spouses always requires recognizing ourselves. It's tough to handle all the material that pops up and sits in the way of actually listening because you've got a lot of emotions and needs prickling at you.

That's why calming down and spending some time interacting with your own feelings and needs is necessary. When you need to do this, be frank with your partner: "I want to understand you, but first I need to sit by myself, will you give me time? It would sound better than not being heard by your partner.

Pay heed to your bodily sensations to fine-tune your feelings and needs. This lets you consciously understand what is happening to you, and you can then discuss it with your spouse. For example, you may consider: "Does your neck or arms hair prickle up? Does your heart race? Do you feel flushed? Will you be controlling your pace carefully? What is it that you need to feel calmer, soothed, and safer? "Our appreciation of our partners requires diligence on our side. It demands that we stop and not disturb our companion or try to formulate responses in our heads. It demands that we shift our complete focus to them. That is not a simple job. So, practice is required. Yet, it still gives a wonderful gift to our partners: the joy of being accepted for who they are and what they deserve.

Couples get together to believe in the idea of happiness. Couples are sticking together as they really feel they will make things work. People in relationships want pretty much the same things: affection, stability, trust.

There is a way to create a better bond, but there's no way to establish it until you completely grasp your partner's inner feelings and such. You may say to yourself: "I understand my wife, of course. She won't let me forget what I need to know about her. "You may think this is understanding, but it's recognized as ignoring something you're sick of listening about. There's something very different from understanding.

The reason the couples complain about each other is that their desires are not being addressed. Those needs differ with every person. One spouse will feel distant from her husband and may want to feel as though she is important to him. If this were revealed to her husband, he might also be able to do anything to make her feel better. It may sound like, "Honey, I'm glad to be with you." It doesn't take anything to fill in what's needed so long as you know what's required. This is comprehension.

Unfortunately, it typically sounds like, when people are upset, "Oh, you didn't pick up the dinner dishes. Why wouldn't you ever take the garbage out? "Such critiques can provide us with an example of the feelings beneath. They can feel neglected and become depressed and then furious, and all those feelings come out of complaints about dinner plates or garbage.

Most of us are not encouraged to explore our inner feelings—those that render us cross with our partners. Then we just take the sorrow and the frustration and turn that into a critique in the expectation that we can at least get something back. Yet, sometimes, the return response becomes worse. Nobody wants to be questioned, and nobody reacts to criticism well. It does hurt. What we find in a lot of marriages is feeling hurt on top of feeling hurt. One party is saying something negative, and the other is replying and putting it on a notch. They still feel betrayed and misunderstood. This might also transform into a habit in which people wind up staying. "It's not that horrible," they might rationalize, but it's not good either.

Many people know how to offer an excuse to overcome hurt feelings. Anything like this could go, "I'm sorry I was rough and said that to you," this helps with bringing the pair back on equal terms before the next bit of misunderstanding, but most people don't even know how to speak to their spouse about what they want, and they end up feeling upset about it.

It may be useful to know what happens within the individual before the assault begins. That's where understanding plays a part. If she realized she wanted to feel valued and respected by her husband, maybe she should ask for it. This may sound like this, "Honey, sometimes in this relationship I feel as though I'm isolated, and it doesn't really matter what I do. I realize that's not the case, but could you please let me know I'm important to you right now?" That's not how people communicate in actual life, so it's awesome to know what you need to for your partner to give that to you. This needs feeling comfortable enough to be vulnerable, and this is a point certain people consider this tough to get to. This is exactly the situation where counseling helps.

If spouses were to know at the moment what their spouse requires, wishes, or desires, they would both be able to give that to him or her. Similar people like to see their spouses satisfied. Couples having a healthy relationship don't want their partners hurting. The important thing is getting people to accept each other and themselves in order to feel satisfied. When couples master this, it's easy to find out.

Try to make your partner aware of this. What is it that he likes, needs, or desires? You will be good to be on the way to a stronger relationship when you know this; one with affection, stability, and, above all, understanding.

There is a reason why comprehending is one of the most important aspects of a good relationship in an interpersonal relationship. This trait not only inspires your companion to be who they choose to be without fear of rejection, but it also allows you to see things from their point of view.

When you're trying to figure out how to be a more caring husband or wife in your relationship, remember to consider and exercise these main characteristics.

Ways to Be More Understanding

There are ways in which a relationship may be more understanding.

Spend Your Time Getting to Know Your Partner

The difficulties in trying to comprehend another human stem from one's unwillingness to really accept them not only as a friend but also as a unique entity capable of a wide range of emotions and feelings. It's difficult to admire anyone because you don't recognize them: their talents, their joys, their fears, and even their flaws. As a couple, you can take your time and get to know your partner better. This could take months or even years, but it would all be worth it if you want the relationship to thrive.

Pay Attention to Your Own Emotions and Motives

It can be difficult to consider another individual because you don't understand yourself. What is your level of familiarity with one another? What causes you to be good, depressed, or angry? What would you do if those thoughts encourage you? How do they assist you in making decisions? When you discover the answers to these questions for yourself, it would be easy for you to look at your partner and recognize their own challenge.

Never Force Your Own Views and Opinions on Others

You are smarter than your partner, no matter how much you consider in terms of experience, intellect, or even maturity. Never impose your own thoughts and values on your mate. You can just be naive and unaware about how they really feel if you do this.

If you want to be an understanding spouse in a relationship, you'll realize that respecting your spouse's beliefs and accepting their own viewpoints as part of who they are is critical.

Enable Your Partner to Have a Life Outside of Your Marriage

Having an accepting partner means realizing that a friendship isn't the center of the world, and your significant other is no exception. To put it another way, don't force your partner to surrender your relationship—which implies giving them the freedom to live and have fun, particularly if you're not present.

Be Considerate of Your Partner's Human Needs

Allow your partner to go out with friends or spend time with family. Allow them to fly alone and live their life to the fullest even though you are away. Overall, enable them to pursue their personal purpose and encourage them to go out into the world to achieve their greatest ambitions.

Keep in Mind That You Are Not Always Right

In terms of the previous segment, becoming an accommodating partner entails listening to what the other person has to offer. You aren't always right, but trying to persuade your partner that your views, feelings, and decisions are more rational will irritate them even more, perhaps leading to a conflict rather than a settlement.

Master the Art of Compromise

If you want to be an accepting spouse, you can work on seeking common ground and agreeing to compromise rather than insisting on being correct all of the time. Since your partner isn't the enemy, you're both fighting the same battle.

Before Saying Anything, Give Your Partner a Chance to Clarify

Allow your partner to justify themselves whether you think they have done something to make you feel upset, annoyed, or sad. Listen to the story from their point of view, and don't pass judgment too quickly. People in relationships sometimes seem to choose anger and tend to disruptive emotional outbursts before speaking with their spouses.

Recognize the Partner's Motivations and Intentions

That knowing how to think is the most challenging thing to do, especially when your spouse has done something wrong, especially if you are angry and betrayed, you must have the confidence and love to care, but with complete sincerity. More importantly, you must preserve your partner's confidence and encourage them to explain their intentions and what prompted them to do so.

Still Choose Goodness Over Anger

In relation to the previous pieces, if you believe your companion to be at fault, you will still try to be kind rather than allowing rage to exacerbate the situation. Anger can never fix anything, particularly if you've done anything that might lead to the end of your relationship.

Anger is a natural reaction to something that affects you, but it's the wrong path to take, particularly if you're trying to save a dying friendship. When trying to make it work, becoming more compassionate entails choosing to be loving and respectful, allowing you to evolve together.

Assist Your Partner in Learning from Their Mistakes

Being understanding is another way to save a relationship that has already been ruined. It will help you heal and remember that, even though your spouse made mistakes, he or she deserves another chance to show himself or herself.

During this process of the relationship, you must play your part in the relationship by helping them understand important other lessons regarding their flaws. You must be cautious and have the ability to do something again if necessary. More importantly, strive to focus on the initiative rather than the mistakes they made.

Encourage Your Partner to Open Up a Little More

Except in a close friendship, not everyone knows how to put their feelings and opinions into sentences. First and foremost, how can you comprehend anyone if they don't know how to express their thoughts and share their deepest feelings? For this situation, you need to be more cautious.

Encourage your spouse to be more open about problems that can directly or indirectly affect your relationship. You'd also have a clear idea about how you'll deal with whatever unforeseen problems you face as a pair on a daily basis.

Understanding Leading Towards a Healthy Relationship?

A relationship is unique, and there are a variety of reasons why people come together. A mutual view of both what you want to be and where you want the relationship to go is part of what makes a healthy friendship. And you'll only discover this if you talk to your mate honestly and openly. However, there are certain features that most happy relationships have in common. Whatever goals you set for yourself or the challenges you face together, knowing these core principles can help you maintain optimistic, rewarding, and exciting relationships.

Maintain a Strong Interpersonal Bond Between You and Your Partner

You help each other feel satisfied and mentally content. Being loving and getting loved are two different things. When you feel cherished, and somebody really understands you, it helps you feel accepted and respected by your partner. Even if the couples are not physically attached to each other, certain couples are stuck in peaceful coexistence. Although the relationship may seem to be good on the surface, a lack of ongoing contact and personal connection just serves to create distance between two people.

You're Not Scared of (Social) Disunity

Some individuals can hash it out in a peaceful manner, whilst others can raise their voices and protest vehemently. The key to a good connection, however, is to not be afraid of conflict. You must be willing to speak out on concerns that affect you without fear of backlash, and you must be able to resolve conflicts without humiliation, disrespect, or a need to be correct.

Outside Relationships and Interests Are Controlled by You

Nobody, whatever the assurances of romantic books or films, will meet any of the needs. In fact, expecting too much from your spouse can put unnecessary strain on your relationship. To encourage and deepen your romantic relationship, maintain relationships with family and friends, and maintain your passions and interests, it is important to maintain your own identity outside of the relationship.

You Communicate Honestly and Openly

Any relationship needs to be able to communicate effectively. It will increase confidence and strengthen the relationship so both parties will understand what they want from the collaboration and will feel comfortable expressing their wishes, interests, and desires.

> **The Difference Between Falling in Love and Staying in Love**

In certain cases, falling in love continues to happen only to some individuals. It takes determination and commitment to stay in love—or to sustain the sensation of "falling in love." The investment, though, is well worth it because of the rewards. In all good and difficult times, a secure, healthy, loving relationship would serve as an everlasting source of comfort and pleasure in your life, strengthening all aspects of your well-being. By taking steps now to preserve or rekindle the feeling of falling in love, you will build a lifelong friendship that will last a lifetime.

Although there are actual, unforeseen challenges to overcome, several couples focus on their relationships. They also turn their attention back to their careers, babies, or other interests after the problems have been resolved. As a result, romantic relationships necessitate a lifetime of commitment and fidelity to a happy union. As far as the well-being of a romantic relationship is important to you, this will include your attention and resources. And now, identifying and addressing small problems in your relationship can aid in preventing it from deteriorating farther down the road. The following tips will help you keep your romantic relationship safe and sustain the sensation of falling in love.

Tip 1: Schedule Face-to-Face Meeting Time

You feel in love as you look at each other and talk to each other. You would be able to maintain the long-term falling-in-love feeling as you choose to search and listen with the same diligence.

You're always thinking of the first moment you saw your significant other. All seem different and interesting, so you spent a lot of time chatting or brainstorming new things to do. However, as time passes, the demands of work, family, other commitments, and the need for time to ourselves can find spending time together more difficult.

Many people have noticed that hurried calls, texts, and text messages are gradually replacing face-to-face contact from their early dating days. While digital communication is convenient for several purposes, it may not have the same beneficial effect on the brain and nervous system as face-to-face communication. It's sweet to send a text or voice mail to your partner saying, "I love you," but if you never smile at them or sit down with them, they'll still think you don't understand or appreciate them. You can have become more distant or alone as a partner. The emotional messages that both of you need to feel loved can only be expressed in person, and it is important to spend time together, no matter how busy your lives are.

Make an Effort to Spend Meaningful Time with Your Partner on a Regular Basis

Take a few minutes per day, no matter how busy you are, to set down your mobile gadgets, stop thinking about other things, and instead focus on and chat with your partner.

Find a Fun Activity That You and Your Partner Will Do Together If it's a popular hobby, a dance lesson, a short walk, or relaxing over a morning cup of coffee, try something interesting.

Do Something Different Together

Doing different stuff together can be a good chance to connect and keep things exciting. It might be as simple as visiting a new restaurant or taking a day trip to a place you've never been before.

Concentrate on Having a Good Time with Your Partner

Couples are often more humorous and friendly in the early stages of a relationship. However, when life's challenges get in the way or old resentments keep piling up, it's easy to lose sight of the good mindset. Maintaining a sense of humor, in particular, will assist you in getting through difficult times, reducing tension, and resolving problems more quickly. Consider thoughtful ways to impress your mate, such as taking roses home or unexpectedly scheduling a place at their favorite restaurant. Playing with pets or small children will even help you bond with your playful side.

Collaborate on Activities That Help Others

Focusing on something outside of your relationship that you and your partner love is one of the most effective ways to stay together and connected. Volunteering with a cause, project, or community service that is important to both of you can keep the friendship fresh and enjoyable. It can also expose you to new experiences and viewpoints, enable you to work together to solve new challenges, and provide you with new opportunities to communicate.

There is immense joy in achieving everything for someone to gain, in addition to helping to relieve agony, fear, and depression. As people and as a couple, humans are hard-wired to help others—the more you support, the happier you do.

Tip 2: Communicate to Stay Connected

A good relationship needs effective communication. When you and your partner have a strong relationship connection, you can feel safe and protected. When people stop interacting well, they stop connected well, and periods of transition or uncertainty will really bring the separation out. It will seem difficult, but as long as you talk, you will be able to overcome the obstacles.

Tell Your Mate Exactly What You Want. Make Sure They Don't Guess

It's not really easy to talk about what you need. For one thing, in a relationship, most of us do not spend enough time communicating about what is really relevant to us. So, even though you know what you need, you might feel nervous, ashamed, or even embarrassed to think about it. However, see it from your partner's perspective. Giving comfort and empathy to everyone you care for is a joy, not a burden.

When you've known each other for a while, you might feel your partner has a good idea of what you're thinking and what you need. Your mate, on the other hand, isn't a mind reader. Although your partner may have an opinion, it is much easier to express your wishes simply to avoid misunderstandings. Your partner may sense something, but it's possible that this isn't what you need. Furthermore, people change, so what you wanted and expected five years ago could be very different now. Instead of causing anger, confusion, or indignation to grow when your partner continues to get it wrong, get in the habit of reminding them exactly what you require.

Pay Attention to the Partner's Non-Verbal Signals

What we don't say expresses much too much about our communication. Eye touch, voice sound, posture, and gestures like bending back, crossing your arms, or taking someone's hand to communicate much more effectively than words. If you can read your partner's nonverbal signs or "body language," you'll be able to see how they really feel and respond accordingly. For a relationship to thrive, each individual must be able to understand their own nonverbal signs as well as their spouse's. Your partner's reactions might vary from yours. For instance, one individual may need a romantic mode of interaction after a stressful day, while another may simply want to go for a walk or relax whilst conversing.

It's important to make sure the body language reflects what you're saying. If you say "I'm good," then clench your teeth and turn away, your face clearly demonstrates that you are far from "usual." When you get positive emotional signals from your spouse, you feel loved and happy, and your spouse feels the same way when you send positive emotional signals. When you refuse to be interested in your own or your spouse's feelings, the relationship between you will deteriorate, and your desire to communicate will suffer, particularly during times of stress.

Be an Active Listener

While our culture places a lot of emphasis on communication, if you can learn to connect in a way that makes another individual feel valued and understood, you can form a deeper, stronger connection. In this case, there is a huge contrast between hearing and truly knowing. You will note the occasional intonations of your companion's accent, telling you how they really sound and the emotions they're trying to express if you consciously listen—because you're interested in what's being addressed. It's not about agreeing with your buddy or shifting your mind to be a better listener. However, it will assist you in identifying unique points of view that will assist you in resolving disagreements.

Control the Stress

When you're stressed or emotionally drained, you're more likely to misread your sexual partner, send confusing or off-putting nonverbal signals, or engage in unacceptable knee-jerk action patterns. How much do you become overwhelmed and go off the handle with a loved one, saying or doing something you then regret? Not only will you be able to tolerate tension more quickly and move to a relaxed atmosphere, but you will still be able to help mitigate tensions and misunderstandings—as well as comfort your partner as tempers rise.

Tip 3: Maintain Physical Intimacy

Touch is an important aspect of human existence. Infant experiments have also shown the importance of daily, affective contact for brain development. And the benefits don't stop when you're a kid. Affectionate touch raises oxytocin levels in the body, a substance that affects communication and connection.

While sex is still a pillar of a healthy relationship, it might not be the only source of sexual interaction. The constant, affectionate contact—keeping hands, hugs, kissing—is also meaningful.

Of course, it's important to be aware of your partner's preferences. Unwanted contact or awkward overtures will make the other party tense and withdraw, which is the last thing you want. That may be attributed to how often you engage with your partner about your interests and emotions like it is with so many other aspects of a good relationship.

If you have to deal with busy job schedules or small children, you can help keep physical affection alive by scheduling daily couple time, whether it's a date night or an hour at the end of the day where you can chill and talk or hold hands.

Tip 4: Learn How to Manage the Give and Take Ratio in Your Relationship

You're setting yourself up for disappointment if you plan to get what you want in a relationship 100 percent of the time. Good relationships are built on compromise. Maintaining an equal exchange of effort, on the other hand, necessitates the participation of each person.

Recognize Your Partner's Priorities

Knowing what your partner represents to you will go a long way toward cultivating reciprocal goodwill and reaching an agreement. On the other hand, it's important that your partner is aware of your interests and that you express them clearly. Spending relentlessly on others at the expense of your own needs can only lead to anger and resentment.

Don't Set Yourself the Target of "Winning"

When you approach your partner with the mindset that stuff must be done your way or otherwise, it would be impossible to find an agreement. This mindset also comes from not having one's basic needs met as a teenager, or it may be the result of years of accumulated resentment in a relationship reaching a breaking point. Having strong views on issues is good, but the partner must still be understood. Be aware of the other person and their point of view.

Learn How to Handle Conflicts in a Friendly Manner

Since conflict is inevitable in any relationship, the partners must feel they are understood in order to sustain a healthy bond. The end aim is to maintain and improve the relationship, not to succeed.

Be Sure You Are Fighting Fairly

Maintain your attention to the problem and have respect for the other guy. Don't start a fight about anything that can't be changed.

Directly Attacking Others Is Not a Good Idea

However, to convey how you feel, use "I" statements. Instead of saying, "You make me feel terrible," claim, "I feel bad when you do that."

Don't Bring up Old Arguments in the Discussion

Rather than focusing on past disagreements or grudges and assigning blame, consider what you might do right now to resolve the issue.

Be Ready to Forgive

It is difficult to end a conflict whether you are unable or unable to forgive anyone.

Take a Break if Tempers Start to Flare

Allow yourself a few minutes to de-stress and calm off before saying or doing anything you'll come to regret. Keep in mind that you're arguing with the one you care about most.

Learn to Let Go

If you can't come to an agreement, choose to disagree. To continue the debate, two people are needed. You may choose to disengage and carry forward if there is a dispute.

Tip 5: Expect Ups and Downs in a Relationship

It's crucial to keep in mind that any relationship has its ups and downs. You're not really going to agree with anything. One spouse may also cope with a dilemma that directly affects them, such as the death of a loved one. Other events, such as job loss or severe health problems, can affect both parties and make interrelationships unlikely. You may have a variety of ideas about managing finances or raising children. Individuals deal with tension in various ways, and misunderstandings can quickly escalate into agitation and anger.

Don't Share Your Complaints with Your Partner

Life's pressures will make us irritated. If you're under a lot of tension, it might sound like a great idea to vent with your friend rather than snap at them. Fighting like this can seem like a release at first, but it eventually ruins the friendship. Find other ways to manage your fear, anger, and resentment in a healthier way.

Attempting to Impose a Solution into Place Will Lead to Many Further Issues

Everyone is going through their own set of problems and struggles. Keep in mind you are part of a unit. You'll get through the tough stretches if you stick together and keep moving forward.

Take a Look Back to the Beginning of Your Relationship

Discuss the events that brought you together, the point at which you began to drift apart, and if you may work together to rekindle the sensation of falling in love.

Be Flexible and Adaptable

Change is unavoidable throughout life, and if you embrace it or resist it, it will occur. Flexibility is essential to adapt to the transitions that often occur in all relationships, and it aids you in evolving together in both good and bad times.

Look Out to Each Other for Support if the Relationship Needs It

Things in a relationship may often become too complicated or intimidating to handle as a couple. Counseling or speaking with a nearby relative or faith leader may help couples strengthen their relationship.

Should You Be the One in the Relationship That is More Understanding?

Most people have a "no more Mr. Nice Guy" attitude when it comes to marriages, which may be negative in the long run. You want a woman to value you in a relationship, but you still need to embrace her for it to be effective. Will you, though, be the more understanding partner in your relationship?

Essentially, we believe the assertion in the query to be incorrect. It's not like one partner in a relationship can be better or less patient than the other. It's why each of you must do your utmost to improve your communication skills. And, in that case, how can you communicate better and make your relationships happier and more successful?

Active Listening

This is a major one. In your relationship, the woman, exactly like you, wants to be understood. She is entitled to know if she is being considered. The primary means of accomplishing this is by effective contact. How should you go about doing that?

It begins with you actively listening to her rather than just waiting for your turn to talk. Then you want to echo what she meant—the emotional meaning of it, what she was talking about. You do that to show her you've been listening, but just to double-check if you've heard what she's said before reacting. Responding to what she hasn't really said will make her seem perplexed, and it will soon deteriorate.

It is time to respond only after all of these points have been done.

Taking Responsibility for the Emotions

It's preferable to speak for yourself rather than how anyone has made you feel. Possession of your feelings—and, by extension, all of your acts—is a good habit to cultivate. It has benefits in a friendship that goes beyond understanding or even better connectivity. Never blame how she made you act on her, no matter how strongly you believe she was the one who did it. Instead, chat about how things make you sound.

Remember

This can be difficult to remember, particularly if it's in the heat of the moment. But bear in mind that you do if you don't want to keep hearing the same points over and over. It will also assist you in making notes or providing one-word updates of items you want to remember as things get heated.

Be Understanding—Whatever That Means for You

For being the most emotionally sensitive, men in relationships are not understanding. That's not, though, a "yes or no" statement. Apparently, it's a scale. Through the relationships, you should continually strive for greater understanding so that it can go smoothly in the future. Do not feel like constructing Rome in one day. Look to changing and improving yourself continuously.

After all, that's what life is about, really. Keeping stuff going along always. It is the core of male self-improvement, and you should use it in the same manner as every other part of your life in a relationship.

Regardless of how perceptive someone is, knowing other people's feelings isn't always easy, particularly in relationships. There are so many explanations of why your partner may feel like he never emotionally knows you. You may not interact well, you may unintentionally be passive hostile, or you may be way too quick to get mad. This may even have anything to do with your partner because they might not be in tune with their emotions and so cannot perceive theirs. Whatever the case might be, feeling misunderstood, particularly in regard to a relationship, is never pleasant.

So, before we venture into all the directions to understand each other more, take a second and focus on your go-to conversation method. "We get emotionally shocked a number of times in relationships, and we just respond, rather than having the time to label how we actually feel and be honest on what we need," dating Coach Corinne Dobbs, says. "We get angry, and we don't realize why we're so mad, so we always want our partner to recognize why we're angry and understand us." Since no one's a mind reader, it's clear that this solution might not help. Slowing down, picking the words, and giving attention to how you are viewed will be a great approach to manage a heated moment. "In other terms, you will really have a constructive dialogue where the aim is to teach each other, rather than being aggressive, frustrated, or crazy," says Dobbas. Here are a couple of other strategies to keep calm, channel your feelings, connect efficiently and, as a result, ideally "get" one another.

Use As Many "I" Statements as Possible

Rule number one: wherever possible, avoid "you" phrases. "People like to argue with expressions like "you still..." or "you never..." which might feel like an allegation, it's more productive to say "I feel upset when you..." instead. This way, the discussion is about how you feel, rather than what your companion might or might not be doing wrong.

Keep It Short and Sweet

While you might be eager to spill all of your concerns in one session, doing so might be completely daunting to your companion and perhaps detrimental. If you have something sensitive to tell, it is best to keep it brief and simple. Otherwise, your companion may get confused with their feelings and tuning them out.

Focus on Understanding Them

If your companion still feels confused, stepping out of their own head and into yours would be hard for them. So, make sure you consider them—what does annoy them, their point of view, etc.—before you attempt to argue on a point. Emotional interaction is a two-way path. Until you attempt to emotionally understand your spouse, it would be impossible for your spouse to try and understand you.

Keep Your Voice Calm

If you're always raising your voice, remaining quiet and knowing each other would really be difficult. So be vigilant with your pace and your tone. "Keeping your voice soft and polite." If it rises, it'll be more challenging for your partner to understand or relate to you.

Pay Attention to Your Body Language

Body language is another aspect that will influence the response of your companion to you and therefore making it more complicated for them to actually "get" what you need. For instance, if you're standing with your arms crossed, you'll look closed off—and maybe even a little guarded. Start calming, first. Keep the body as relaxed and comfortable as possible while attempting to convey complicated emotions.

Make Emotions Part of Your Daily Conversation

When you two aren't in the habit of expressing emotions, a perfect way to initiate is to build an atmosphere where talking about feelings is totally OK. So, one way to do this is to ask open-ended questions to them. "So instead of asking things like, 'How was your day?' consider something like, 'what was the best thing about your day, and why?' as it encourages your partner to express more. That can help expressing feelings sound natural, and you will have more productive discussions going forward.

Be Clearer About How You Feel

Try to be straightforward and to the point rather than being passive hostile or hinting about what you need and hoping your partner would pick on. You might suggest something straightforward like, "If you glance at your screen all the time, I feel like I'm not important to you. Without your cell, I'd just spend more time being with you. Would you want to be less on your screen while we're together?" It covers four things: what's troubling you, how you feel about it, what'd make you feel better, and whether or not you'd feel better. "And though the proposal is not feasible for your partner, you are going to require consideration of the topic at hand. 8. Don't Criticize or Ask Them to Change

Resist the temptation to clutter your discussion with complaints or suggestions for improvement and keep it all about your emotions instead. It's crucial to concentrate on expressing your own perspective while thinking about emotions because you're either searching for, learning, or understanding—not something else. Whether there is a suggestion for improvement or criticism connected to expressing your own feelings, personal awareness would be distracting.

Tell Them They Don't Need to *Fix* Anything

It is totally natural for partners to switch into "fix it mode because it is painful to see someone we care about so distressed. So that will place a lot of pressure on the other significant person (even though it is a self-imposed strain), and it can make you feel like they aren't listening.

That's why you would want to try to reassure your mate that they don't have to give any suggestions right from the beginning. Tell the person they should not want to make you feel better, but only want them to acknowledge how you feel.

Be Smart Regarding When You Decide to Open Up

Choose the time carefully because you decide to get a heart-to-heart, and always sound comprehensible. "It's not a perfect moment to speak up while the significant partner is half asleep, struggling to reach a job deadline, battling traffic, or enjoying a movie or television show they're focusing on. Chats during car rides may be perfect as they don't involve scheduled discussions or frequent eye contact, any of which may render an individual anxious.

Figure Out How to Speak Their *Language*

Not everyone communicates the same way, and you're going to want to find out how your partner communicates and whilst still making them understand how you communicate. There is a clear difference between the inability to learn and the lack of attention or care.

Try To Connect When Only You're Not Feeling Emotional

When you feel misunderstood, the middle of a heated debate isn't the time to put things that way. Ironically, the only way to get your mate to personally respond to you is to restrict how intensely you are feeling right now. Sometimes a significant other may go through their own fight-or-flight mode when confronted with a highly emotional spouse, particularly if they believe the relationship is in danger. When you're still in the intensely charged state, so little gets heard or conveyed.

Do Not Feel Afraid to Take Some Time Out for Your Partner

When things get tense and you don't feel listened to, don't be scared to stop on the discussion and reconvene later on. "Notice what's going on within your body? Is your heart pounding too fast? Does your skin feel hot? Are you running through the same words in your mind? Take a break, walk away, concentrate on something new for a couple of minutes, and relax back into your body.

Say It in Letter Form

When you feel like you're not willing to bring your feeling into sentences, why not pursue a different format? Start writing as a means of describing your partner's emotionally intense issues in a way you can articulate them accurately. It will allow you some time to think about what you'd like to tell and offer your companion time to read and respond.

Maintain Reasonable Expectations

Bear in mind; if you two are not on the same page right now, it's totally OK. "People have varying personal backgrounds, and not everyone resonates with everyone." A partner may not really appreciate or understand the experience you have. If your companion isn't very comfortable with their own personal background, it's much more doubtful they won't 'notice' yours. Think of emotional understanding as a target to aspire for. "Just keep communicating, no matter what. That's the secret to truly knowing each other and to more effectively share feelings.

CHAPTER 6

STRATEGIES TO OVERCOME ANXIETY, NEGATIVITY, AND JEALOUSY IN A RELATIONSHIP

This chapter will help you to cope with the anxiety, negativity, and jealousy in a relationship. Easy-to-follow strategies are discussed so that the relationship can survive for a lifetime. People with poor self-esteem
are more anxious about marriages, which may make it difficult for them to reap the benefits of a romantic relationship. People with poor self-esteem not only want their friends to see them in a more favorable way than they see themselves, but they often have trouble recalling their partner's affirmations while they are

feeling down. Furthermore, acting on our fears will send a companion apart, resulting in a self-fulfilling prophecy.

Overcoming Anxiety

Since this conflict is interpersonal and occurs much of the time, regardless of circumstances, it's important to address our fears without distorting or dragging our partner into them. We can accomplish this in two steps:

- Fight an invisible enemy that is sabotaging the relationship
- Discover the true sources of anxiety

What Causes Us to Be Stressed?

A distant hurt is reawakened by nothing more than an intimate bond. Rather than anything else, our marriages have triggered old feelings from our past. And our brains are packed with the same neurochemicals in any situation.

We also have relationship models that we learned from strong caregivers during our early attachments. Our early behavior would have an effect on our adult relationships. What partners we choose and the dynamics that play out in our relationships are determined by our attachment style. A consistent pattern of interaction helps an individual feel more at ease and self-assured. Anyone in an anxious or worried relationship, on the other hand, might be more likely to worry about their partner.

It's crucial to consider the relationship category because it'll help us see that we might repeat a trend from our past experiences. This will assist us in selecting better wives and forming deeper relationships, thus improving our sort of relationship. Finally, it can allow us more aware of how our fear, which is based on the past rather than the current, may be skewed.

Anxiety is often caused by a "powerful inner voice" that we have internalized as a result of our past negative behavior. For instance, we try to internalize the point of view and keep it within our heads like a cruel coach, whether we have a parent who hated himself or who led pessimistic behaviors toward us. This inner critic continues to be very vocal about topics that are important to us, such as our marriages. The critical inner voice then ignited doubts about the trust the spouse had in him, and it turned on him. The second time, he viewed the situation through the prism of his delicate inner ear, which convinced him his partner was walking backward, her head overflowing with horrible thoughts about him. He was good for about a minute. The next minute, he was listening to an imagined voice telling him that he couldn't measure up and why he'd been shot.

Relationships are in jeopardy. They put our basic feelings for ourselves to the test and force us out of long-held comfort zones. We keep turning up the volume on our inner voice and reopening old wounds from our past. When we've been ignored as children, a romantic partner's aloof behavior would not just be irritating. It has the ability to transport us back to the emotional state of a scared child seeking safety from our mother. As intimidating as it can seem to match our current responses with our early-life beliefs, behaviors, and expectations, it is a valuable guide for getting to know ourselves and ultimately confronting trends that don't mirror us or really fit our real adult lives.

What Do You Do if You're Worried About Your Relationship?

To challenge our fear, we must first get to know our inner speech. We would continue to grasp it when it falls into our heads over time. It can be straightforward at times. We get all dolled up for a date, and it says, "You have a bad appearance! You're all overweight. Simply conceal yourself. He'll never get near enough to you." Sometimes, it can be more subdued, even soothing. "Please hold your thoughts to yourself. So that you don't get hit, don't interfere or show her how you feel." This voice can even transform our partner, who makes us much more nervous "You can't put your faith in him. He's clearly having an affair with you!" To begin challenging the critical inner voice, you must first understand it. You will find specific steps to take to defeat this inner adversary and prevent him from infiltrating your romantic life here.

We will begin to act in ways that are counter to the guidance of our essential inner mind if we continue to challenge these destructive views of ourselves. In terms of a friendship, this means not acting out based on unfounded insecurities or reacting in ways we don't respect. Here are a few steps to get you started:

Maintain Your Liberty

It's important to have a sense of self separate from our partner. A relationship's aim should be to create a fruit salad rather than a smoothie. To put it another way, we shouldn't ignore crucial aspects of ourselves in order to integrate with a mate. Rather, as we go on, each of us will seek to uphold the unique aspects of ourselves that first brought us together. We should continue to grow in this direction, realizing that we are full beings in and of ourselves.

Don't Overreact, No Matter How Anxious You Are

Of course, it's easier said than achieved, but we all realize that our fears can lead to some very harmful behavior. Acts of jealousy or possessiveness can injure our mate, as well as ourselves. We can stop calling every few minutes, snooping through their text messages to see where they are and what they're up to, and being enraged every time they smile at a gorgeous girl, no matter how anxious it makes us, so we'll be way happier and more relaxed in the end. Furthermore, we must be trustworthy.

Since we can only change our half of the equation, it's therefore worth considering if there are certain actions, we do that push our partner apart. When we see anything, we want but don't think we merit it, we can make a conscious attempt to talk to our companion about it or change the situation, so we don't feel betrayed or allow ourselves to act in ways we don't like.

Do Not Look for Reassurance

When we are nervous, we run to our partner for warmth, which just adds to our weakness. These patterns come from within ourselves, and no matter how brilliant, lovely, noble, or attractive our partner tells us that we are, we will not be able to overcome them until we can conquer them within ourselves. Whatever the case might be, we can strive to feel positive for ourselves. This entails fully accepting our spouse's affection and devotion towards us. However, that should not mean that we can look to our partner for reassurance on some basis to make sure we're okay since this place more responsibility on our partner and takes attention away from ourselves.

Stop Calculating

It's important that we don't over-analyze or evaluate any move our partner produces. We must acknowledge that our partner is a sovereign-minded person of a different mindset. We won't always perceive things the same way or express our emotions in the same way. This isn't to say that we'd settle for anyone who doesn't offer us anything we desire in a relationship; rather, if we find someone we love and appreciate, we'll try and avoid falling into a titfor-tat trap in which we constantly quantify who owes whom and when.

A friendship will be equitable in terms of complexity and goodwill distribution. When anything doesn't sound right, we can articulate ourselves plainly, but we don't want our friends to read our minds or know exactly what to do all of the time. It's impossible to break out from the blame game after we've fallen behind it.

Put All on the Line

We all experience anxiety, so by being frank with ourselves, we will improve our sensitivity to the many ambiguities that a developing relationship can inevitably pose. Even if we know an individual has the potential to harm us, we should invest in them. Holding one foot out the door keeps the engagement as close as it can be and can also end it. We are expected to feel insecure if we allow ourselves to be cherished and embraced but holding it out has more advantages than we might imagine. When we take a chance and don't let our fears control our decisions, the best-case scenario is that the relationship blossoms, and the worst-case scenario is that we evolve inside ourselves. There hasn't been a shortage of time that has taught us a lot about ourselves and nurtured our capacity to love and be vulnerable.

Overcoming Negativity

Negativity in relationships causes conflicts between couples, such as violence, abandonment, infidelity, lack of trust, etc. They both lack interest in each other and the relationship, leaving their future ambiguous as a couple.

Neglecting Your Partner

The most significant aspect of a relationship is the development of companionship and being around one another. Once we start offering our attention to other hobbies and desires than our partner, this gives rise to problems of neglect, which may trigger ups and downs in the relationship.

Not Being Attentive Towards Your Partner

It is not enough to be present there. If there are no feelings in it, the relationship does not last. To be there, also be able to express your affection and respect for your partner. Tell yourself in both physical and emotional ways.

Being Dishonest

Those five letters T-R-U-S-T describe the base of your relationship. In every relation, it is the most important element. Lying and infidelity destroy the bond between two people. Cheating will create significant complications, so partners are encouraged to consult in order to navigate through this season.

Physical Abuse

Aggressive behavior is never appropriate, especially when the interaction contributes to abuse. Physical, mental, or sexual violence destroys relationships and families and in relationships gives rise to toxic energies. Ensure that the toxic partner is involved in conflict management programs.

And if the behavior does not improve, it is easier to withdraw from this relationship.

Gossiping

It's good to chat about your marriage issues with your mates and family, whether you still explore the solutions. Yet if it's a mere conversation, then it's considered gossip that gives marriage negativity. Your wife might feel cheated, for example, that you leaked confidential and intimate details to others. Your partner may even find gossiping an emotional scam.

Putting Yourself Last

"Nice guys also end last" is a phrase that has started to make a lot of sense for the men and women who are committed. Martyrs are uncommon individuals, and they are always furious, resentful, and disappointed. It does not mean to be inconsiderate and show no concern for others. When you wish to live and develop a good relationship, so you do need to fulfill your needs. Make sure you are viewed with dignity by people; if you function like a doormat, you encourage hostility in your relationship. Stand up for yourself, and protest if you feel disrespectful. Respect yourself almost as much as your spouse does.

10 Ways to Keep Negativity Away from Your Relationships

1. Have Open Lines of Communication

Healthy relationships need direct, uninhibited communication; if the people in it hold secrets and shut themselves off having actual discussions, no relationship will last for long. Relationships will take a turn for the worst easily if people start distancing themselves and will not accept that the other person has done anything or said anything to annoy them. Nonetheless, when you threaten somebody, you will always respond rationally and hold a civilized dialog that doesn't result in screaming and shouting at each other's names.

Only note that a good relationship is founded on honesty and clear communication, and if you want to prevent conflict, seek to foster both in all your close relationships.

2. Don't Pick Apart the Other Person's Flaws

A sure-fire way to begin disputes and wreck a relationship is to nit-pick and put somebody's imperfections in their face. Note that each individual may have attributes under the skin, but such attributes will not make up the entirety of who they are. Bear in mind, though, that you certainly have characteristics that bother some people, but your near friends and family might not find it a point to blame you about them. They embrace you exactly the way you are, the defects, and all.

When you don't particularly like the company of someone, you should let the relationship go without tearing down the other individual – just come clean to them and reassure them tactfully that you think it will help all of you to go your separate ways.

3. Appreciate One Another

If it's your co-worker, partner, relative, mom, or dad, let the individual realize that from time to time, you appreciate them. Everybody in life deserves to feel valued, and then they feel like they've made a difference in this world. If you consider and compliment somebody's good qualities, they would be motivated to perceive you in the same way.

Optimistic relationships require both partners to have affection, commitment, and reciprocal respect. Every time you see your mate, your co-worker, your family, and so forth, let them realize that you love them and how much you truly respect them.

4. Don't Hold onto Relationship Grudges

Everyone is making mistakes, so that doesn't mean they need to be kept above their heads for their entire lives. Accept that from time to time, humans make errors and forgive the individual for the mishap. Of course, if someone wanted to harm you deliberately, you would need to handle it a little differently, but most people don't go out of their way to inflict another person's pain. It was actually just an innocent error because, at some stage, no person on Earth would really go through their whole lives without messing up.

Know you have made errors in the past, too, so you will not like anyone to continually remind you of your shortcomings too.

5. Leave Jealousy at the Door

Everybody in life has a specific direction, and some may appear to have more or do better than you do. That doesn't suggest you can equate yourself to them and feel bad simply because everything you haven't accomplished has been achieved by them.

What about the race you finished up without your friend? What about the holidays you took a couple of years earlier that your friends asked you they had dreamed about taking?

Don't let jealousy take control of you, for it will deprive you of pleasure and influence your judgments. Bear in mind all of the great interactions and successes that might not be under your belt – that can help put everything in perspective and make you happier with others rather than envy them.

6. Don't Fall into the Destructive Habit of Complaining

Many people view their time together as an excuse for throwing all their life problems onto each other and dissipating their grievances. After the encounter, this leaves both individuals feeling exhausted and uninspired, which opens the way for further conflict in the future. Instead of arguing about issues, think about alternatives.

Note the good stuff in life and pick one another up. Healthy relationships are perfect when both people feel happier rather than bitter.

7. Don't Compare Your Relationship to Others

Every relationship is unique and beautiful; the relationship with your buddy would look different from the relationship with anyone else, so enjoy it for what it is. When you just crave what you don't have, you can never have good relationships and respecting the wonderful bond you share.

8. Don't Try to Change People

Respect people at this moment for whoever they are, rather than coercing them to adjust for your own gain. People will only improve if they want to, so just concentrate on what you value about them, rather than blaming them for their flaws. If they believe you in having to adjust, you may kindly find out a direction for them to improve, but don't take it upon yourself to mandate that they do.

9. Bring Kindness to the Relationship

They would be more likely to demonstrate caring and affection for you if you express love for the other person. Be one like what you expect to see in the world, and your relationship will thrive because you will draw others with the same passion that you already do.

10. Laugh More

If you have plenty to laugh about, it's hard to be pessimistic, so share jokes or go on a lovely holiday with family, mates, colleagues, or your partner. Allow your inner kid to come out and play in the midst of life's seriousness, then not only do you become more light-hearted and happier, but the fun will also put you back together and disperse stress.

Overcoming Jealousy

How to Deal with Jealousy

No one wants to be jealous. But jealousy is an inherent feeling that can be felt in every single one of us. The trouble with jealousy is not that from time to time, it shows up, nor what it brings to us when we don't get hold of it. Experiencing what occurs when we enable our jealousy to overtake us or influence the way we feel about ourselves and everyone around us may be terrifying. This is why knowing where our competitive emotions really come from and discovering how to cope with jealousy in positive, constructive ways is key to so many facets of our lives, from our intimate interactions to our jobs to our personal ambitions.

Why Are We So Jealous, then?

Research has shown predictably that increased jealousy correlates with lower self-esteem. "Most of us are still oblivious of the underlying guilt that resides inside us, for it comes too easily to speak of ourselves with self-critical feelings. Yet, the degree to which we feel jealous and insecure in the present can be heavily influenced by guilt from our experience. The 'critical voice inside' is a type of negative self-talk. This perpetuates negative thoughts and emotions, with intense attention pushing us to evaluate, measure, and judge ourselves (and also others). This is one explanation of why it's so important to know how to cope with jealousy.

This voice will intensify our feelings of jealousy, with negative and malicious comments flooding our minds. In reality, what our vital inner voice informs us regarding our condition is always more complicated to deal with than the actual circumstance. A rejection or alienation by our mate is hard, but all the horrible stuff our sensitive inner voice informs us about ourselves after the incident is what really pains us even more. "You're such an insane person. Have you ever felt you should truly be happy? "You're going to end up lonely. You can never trust someone again. "Take a deeper look at two forms of jealousy to explain how this inner adversary fuels our bad emotions about jealousy: romantic jealousy and competitive jealousy. Although these two types of jealousy sometimes intersect, individually understanding them can help us understand better how jealous feelings can influence various areas of our lives and how we can best cope with jealousy.

Romantic Jealousy

It is a simple fact that relationships get better because individuals don't get unnecessarily jealous. The longer that we will hang onto our jealous emotions and make sense of them apart from our mate, the happier we would be. Note, our jealousy also stems from our own fear – a sense that we are destined to be betrayed, harmed, or rejected. Unless we cope with this feeling inside ourselves, in every relationship, no matter what the circumstances, we are likely to fall prey to feelings of jealousy, mistrust, or insecurity.

Such pessimistic thoughts towards ourselves derive from very early life experiences. We also bear upon ourselves emotions that our parents or significant relatives have towards us or against themselves. In our current relationships, then, unintentionally, we repeat, reconstruct, or respond to old, familiar dynamics. For instance, if we felt set out as children, we might easily interpret our spouse as dismissing us. We may select a spouse who is more difficult or even adhere to actions that will drive away from our spouse.

The degree to which we, as adolescents, inherited self-critical attitudes also affects how much our critical inner voice can influence us in our adult lives, particularly in our relations. And, no matter what our particular perceptions may be, to some degree, we all hold this inner criticism. Most of us can contribute to bringing a sensation that we are not going to be chosen. The degree to which we think this insecurity impacts the way we feel insecure in a relationship.

Lurking behind the anger towards our spouses or questioning a perceived danger from third entities are also serious thoughts about ourselves. Thoughts saying, "What is he seeing in her?" It can easily transform into "She is so much more pretty/thinner/successful than I am!" Even as our worst suspicions come to life when we hear about the affair of a spouse, we always respond by turning frustration to ourselves as being "foolish, unlovable, destroyed, or unwelcome." Like a sadistic teacher, our vital inner voice warns us not to trust or feel too weak. It tells us that we are not lovable and that we are not fit for romance. It is the soft whisper which spreads cynicism, distrust, and confusion. "Why would she work tardy? "Why does he prefer over me, his friends? "What does she do while I'm away? "Why is it that he gives too much attention to what she says? "Those of us who are acquainted with how jealousy functions realize that far too frequently such feelings gradually tend to sprout and blossom into even bigger, more entrenched assaults on oneself and/or our partner. "She's trying to hang around you. Somebody else has to be there." "He is losing interest. He wants to run away from you." "Who will listen? You are too dull. "At some stage in a relationship, this insecure feeling will emerge, from the first date to the twentieth year of marriage. We listen to our inner critic in an effort to defend ourselves and step back from being close to our spouse. And we still seem to be more competitive of an absolute trap after we've withdrawn from doing what we want. If we realize at any level that we don't consider our relationship a focus or consciously follow our aim of being near or caring, we continue to feel more vulnerable and jealous. That's why knowing how to cope with jealousy is much more relevant, and not acting unconsciously on jealous feelings by driving our spouse farther apart.

Competitive Jealousy

Although it can sound futile or illogical, having what others have and feeling jealous is totally normal. Whether we interpret those emotions, though, is quite important to our fulfillment and enjoyment point. This is simply a negative trend of demoralizing consequences because we use these emotions to support our inner rivals, to break down ourselves or others. However, if we don't encourage such emotions to fall through the hands of our vital inner voice, we will potentially use them to understand what we desire, to be more goal-driven, or just to experience more self-acceptance of what influences us.

It's all right, also positive, to let ourselves have a competitive mindset. It can feel amazing when we just let ourselves get the momentary sensation without any decision or action plan. But, if we ruminate or distort this thinking into self-criticism or an assault on another human, we get hurt at it. If we consider ourselves being overreacted or plagued by our thoughts of jealousy, we should do a few things.

Tips to Overcome Jealousy

Be Aware of What Gets Triggered

Think of the different things that make you feel worked up. Is it a friend who has financial success? An ex-partner who dates someone else? A friend who speaks her mind in meetings?

Ask Yourself for What Critical Inner Voices Come Up

What kinds of thoughts spark competitive feelings? Are you using jealous emotions to bring yourself down? Do they make you feel weak, incompetent, ineffective, etc.? Is there a sequence or pattern that seems familiar to those thoughts?

Ponder About the Deeper Implications and Origins of These Thoughts

Do you sense a certain urgency to get something done? Is there something that you think you should be? What does that entail for you to obtain this thing? Does that refer to your past?

When we have asked these questions to ourselves, we may appreciate how such emotions may have more to do with unresolved problems inside ourselves than with our current life or the individual; our jealousy is aimed at. For ourselves, we should show more patience and seek to abandon the prejudices that cause us to feel unhappy.

How to Stop Being a Jealous Companion

If you let jealousy go unregulated, the relationship would decline. It needs trust for yourself and your partner to realize how to avoid being a competitive wife or husband. Get to the root of your jealousy and build a healthier relationship.

Be Honest About Jealousy's Impact

You can't fix a dilemma because you refuse to consider it. Be real instead of claiming that you are not jealous or that your jealousy is not a problem. How are you feeling, and how are they affecting your relationship because of your insecurities?

Recognizing the issues that your jealousy is creating might be complicated but take pride in the fact that you are making the first move towards a stronger relationship.

Ask What Your Jealousy is Telling You

Instead of seeing jealousy as a problem, see your jealousy as a solution. Jealousy (or some other query about relationships) is a window of insight that we should gaze into and achieve clarification. Instead of turning off the jealous behavior right away, seek first to grasp the behavior. What issue is the jealousy attempt to overcome? If you feel jealous that your companion has violated your trust, perhaps the real issue is the lack of trust. It is your insecurities that require consideration if you pass your insecurities into your spouse. If you feel jealous of the achievements of your partner, maybe there is an inappropriate competitive aspect that needs to be removed. Whatever the source, it can help you get to the root of how to avoid getting jealous in a relationship by looking at jealousy as a "solution" and going back from there. To find permanent relief, you will fix it by moving to the real issue.

List Your Insecurities

Looking at yourself begins by learning how to avoid being a jealous husband or wife. What sort of fear causes your jealousy? Is it because of perfectionism you are uncertain of yourself? Would you equate yourself to other people? You don't make this statement yourself to blame-you own your part in the relationship.

Cultivate Self-Confidence

If you have worked up a list of the insecurities that cause your jealousy, write down a solution for each one of them-. When you remain in the shadow of an ex-partner, make a compilation of all the qualities that your spouse likes in you. If you are always contrasting yourself to celebrities, unfollow them for a week on Instagram. You'll be able to build the self-confidence you need to conquer jealousy by allowing yourself space from feelings of inferiority.

Consider the Source of Your Insecurity

Mastering how to avoid jealousy in a relationship is also a question of treating past wounds. If you deal with jealousy because of an underlying condition such as childhood abuse or addiction, get the help you need to tackle it. You will turn your conflicts into sources of power with the right support.

Be Honest with Your Partner

When you are dealing with jealousy, your partner has undoubtedly recognized it too. Most likely, your partner will also help the situation. Through actively collaborating, you appreciate your commitment when keeping your partner committed as well – and offer them the chance to help you while you seek a solution.

Build Healthy Coping Skills

Even in a relationship, it can be difficult to let go of jealousy if you don't have a more positive way to connect. If your partner does not give you a justification to feel paranoid or jealous (i.e., by cheating on you or lying frequently), it is up to you to suppress your jealousy trigger. Recognize you don't need to feel jealous – you're already used to that. Care for yourself to nurture your physical, emotional, and mental wellbeing. These become the routine as you emphasize positive coping strategies, which ultimately eliminate jealousy.

Dissolving the feelings of rage and jealousy in relationships requires shifting the underlying values about fear and unconscious expectations about what the mate is doing.

The steps to completely end jealous reactions are:

- **Recovering emotional influence** so you can regain charge of your thoughts to stop reactive behavior.
- **Shift your point of view** so that in your mind, you may move back from the plot. This should allow you a time span to stop a jealous or angry response to do something else.
- **Identify** the core beliefs which activate the emotional response.
- **Be mindful** that your mental convictions aren't valid. That is distinct from scientifically "knowing" that the tales are not real.
- **Establish the power** of your concentration, and you can choose deliberately which tale is unfolding through your subconscious and which feelings you experience.

There are a number of elements that establish jealousy dynamics. As such, successful approaches would have to tackle various aspects of values, opinions, desires, and willpower. When you skip one or more of these factors, then you leave the path open to revert to certain negative feelings and behaviors.

You will move back from the narrative by doing a few basic exercises, which project the mind and withdraw from the emotional response. When you just want to alter your thoughts and behavior, only you should achieve it. Training valuable knowledge requires only the desire. You can find useful techniques and activities to conquer the internal jealousy response.

Principle envy factors are assumptions that cause feelings of anxiety Feelings of low self-esteem are centered on perceptions that we have in a conceptual picture of who we are. We don't have to adjust to remove the fear and low self-esteem; we only have to shift our confidence in the delusional self image. While certain may believe that this may be tough, it is just daunting because most may not have acquired the requisite skills to alter a conviction. When you learn the techniques, you realize it requires very little time to alter a conviction. You just avoid involving yourself in the tale. It needs more time to believe something than not to believe it.

CHAPTER 7

SELF-EVALUATION

How to evaluate yourself in a relationship and the methods to do so are discussed in this chapter. Questions for the evaluation and dimensions upon which one should try to improve are also discussed. Here's why

self-assessment is essential for healthy relationships

If you could date yourself, do you think you'd be satisfied and pleased with the marriage or the relationship?

Would You Date Yourself?

When you're single and ready for a relationship, but nothing appears to fall out, there's a temptation to find yourself, see your fantastic attributes and pretty features, and believe that you're good, and it's only for a right moment when someone amazing comes along.

Yet, then, is it going to be a question of time or of change?

Perhaps the singularity is not so much a perception problem as it is a self-delusion concern. What if you're not always as smart as you let yourself believe? What if you're just doing great but always fall shy of the criteria required to attract the kind of man or woman you've seen in your mind?

You know, it's easy to conjure in your head the vision of a perfect partner, but it's not that straightforward to have an acceptable visual image of yourself. This would not be that easy to agree, perhaps. You may also not be as cool as you believe you are.

If and that's why it's necessary to ask yourself the introspective question honestly-' would I date myself? 'And still, create painfully frank self assessment if you do so. That should, by the way, be very regular.

That could be where the secret for you to find a partner lies. There is a persistent need for self-assessment, particularly among people who are currently dating and others who are still married, to continuously see one's self through the simple lens of candid introspection.

You will be realistic and selfless enough to question yourself; if he or she behaves this way, would I be satisfied with my partner? Should I feel happy with them handling me like this? Would I really blame them for this kind of behavior?

Whether there are any moral defects in you that anyone else will never tolerate, don't be selfishly deluded into believing they'd take that from you.

This is not the way it functions. When you wouldn't want it, bring yourself to work on it and genuinely aspire to grow more. Not only has your [potential] partner needed this.

Repeatedly, by doing so, you are becoming a stronger version of yourself up to the point that you become comfortable enough to respond in the affirmative when you are asked: "Should you date yourself? "It's not that convenient to be self-analytical as it appears. That's why the self-assessment report you've got to do at work is already sitting on your desk waiting to conclude.

So that sort of self-analysis is important while you are in a relationship. What can you do to boost your relation? What do you need to bring in there from your husband or wife?

If you're prepared to go deep into your own brain to improve your relationship's wellbeing, here's where to start:

Learn How to Pick Up on Your Own Patterns

If you want to make a difference in your to-do list in your everyday life, serious consideration will slip to the bottom of your priorities. This is why it's necessary to set aside time and take a look back to see if your actions relate to your relationship (both positive and negative). Journaling is a perfect opportunity to get a snapshot of the acts you perform and the thoughts you keep on revisiting.

Don't Be Afraid to Over-Communicate

You don't want to undermine the intellect of your spouse, and you believe that out of your relationship, they realize what you expect and need. Yet you know what they're doing about presuming—it's real. And if it seems your desires are clear, don't be shy to ask your boyfriend or girlfriend, to be precise. Let them know just how they can make you feel relaxed and comfortable.

Be Generous with Your Praise

When your significant other is doing anything less than perfect, it's easy to get cynical, so if you're going to judge, you ought to be able to take constructive feedback. Consider the effect "yelp." Most people just dream about writing a comment when they've had a terrible restaurant encounter, so when it's all peachy, they just go ahead with their day. Make it a point to praise your boo as well as condemn it positively. You are loving how they made dinner while you were having an especially stressful day? Admire the expertise in preparing their trip? Let's just let them know.

Don't Immediately Reject Criticism

Hearing criticism may be difficult, particularly when it comes from someone you love, but this support is important if the relationship is to be further strengthened. When your companion gives you thoughts on what they need, be open to the input and ready to adapt when necessary.

Don't Let Outside Stresses Put Extra Pressure on Your Relationship

A celebration is coming up. If this individual is "The one" or if/when you get married, you feel this constant stress. All of a sudden ordinary talk appears to get even more complex, and in all, you are trying to seek a secret context. It will draw on a close relation and make it uncomfortable. When you're an adult, outdoor tension comes with the territory, so make it a point to accept your relationship for what it is. Don't allow relatives, friends, or other influences to put pressure on you and trigger stress and spill through your relationship.

Self-Evaluation and Preparation for Relationship Success

Self-evaluation can be difficult, but the benefits can be fantastic. When a self assessment is done and the results present, the probability of you gaining a relationship of greater quality than you have in the past significantly increases.

Preparation for Success

Preparedness to be in a relationship is essential for its survival. When you're not ready, you're likely to mess things up or indulge in a poor relationship. Even worst, as they step into your world, you won't know the right one. An accurate self-assessment will disclose any shortfalls.

Preparation will continue with a self-assessment. Have you evolved into the type of person in your heart you know you should be? Is your life on track? Is it in equilibrium? An individual starting the path cannot be in a state of need or loss for his ideal life partner. They'll need to be secure and stable. Otherwise, they'll be in a relationship that represents their inappropriate state of life.

This self-evaluation includes looking at the four main fields where relationships appear to have the most influence: emotional, physical, social, and financial.

Emotional

Have you achieved emotional maturity, or are you already holding lingering trauma from a previous hurtful relationship or a traumatic childhood? If so, first get it settled! Speak to a buddy, read any books about self-help, or visit a therapist or clergy.

Have you mastered your subconscious by taking care of your thought content? Have you learned of your emotions' incredible strength and how they decide your attitude, physiology, and fate? If not, purchase some books, tapes, or attend a lecture on the matter. Then use the knowledge to build your intellectual strength to use your emotions to function for you instead. It is important to become an expert in this field, as it will influence almost every aspect of your life, including your capability to find a spouse who is right for you.

Have you made up a list of core beliefs and short and long-term goals? If not, then do now! Write down the principles and the goals. Give it a path to your future. Create a roadmap for the life you dream of and the person you desire to be along the way.

Physical

Are you happy with your appearance, dietary habits, and training program? It doesn't mean that when you continue your journey, you need to be at your perfect weight, fitness routine, or food schedule. But this does suggest you need a full embrace and respect for your body.

If not, take steps immediately to reduce weight, begin a regimen of exercise, and set up a diet plan. Only taking the pledge and being frank will be what it takes for you to achieve self-acceptance.

Yet don't deceive yourself because the mental boost of making the first major move in completing a weight-reduction plan, purchasing a gym card, or signing up for a fitness course would just be fleeting. You have to carry the job through and stick with it. It takes about six weeks to develop a new habit, experts claim. This period of time will be a fair beginning of stamina, contributing to the outcomes you expect.

Social

It's necessary to have social equilibrium in a relationship. Finally, exclusive dependence on a mate for all of your social nourishment and comfort will place so much burden on a relationship. It can also significantly limit its potential to satisfy.

Even social interactions that exist outside a relationship may achieve some elements of personal fulfillment. Participation in social events that meet mutual desires, such as belonging to a common community group, will provide the social stimulation needed by each partner. And, unless social conditions are fulfilled, the relationship as a couple becomes significantly beneficial if they're not, so it becomes a misery.

Friendships of your own sex people are often essential to a relationship's progress. There are certain things that only someone of their own gender will grasp. It is not fair to close yourself off from the rest of the world and to ask your companion to accept all the problems that come with being a male or a female. Relying solely on them for advice on these things won't satisfy all of your needs. And the outcome when they are unable to satisfy them is disappointment, aggravation, and turmoil.

The relation a person has with their (same sex) mates is not a substitution for the intimate bond you share as a couple. It just strengthens it, and even to a significant degree, it does so! Men are consolidating themselves as men through interacting with other guys. Women continue improving themselves as women by bonding with other females. Then, there are romantic sparks as two spiritually replenished couples sync.

Financial

No other single problem tends to break more relationships than financial matters. It's disrespectful to your partner and yourself to get into a relationship without your finances being in order. Just as in all the other aspects we mentioned above, it is important that you both be safe in this field so that your relationship is based on a solid basis, not on the sand, and definitely not on quicksand.

Are the accounts in balance then? Would you have the power of your payment cards and other payment-producing areas? How is your tax and savings planning? Should you take full advantage of occupational retirement insurance programs? Would you set up a personal investment program? If not, then have it done this instance! Of all, if you want to get them, do you not want to be a provider to the future of you and your partner and that of your children? Clearly, your employment standing plays a key role in your financial wellbeing.

Will you have a successful career? It doesn't say you have to be at your ideal workplace, but then you have to be happy in your current position or move for your target in another way. So, you're taking classes at a nearby college or trade school, for example, or you're interested in a promotion for your own new job or company.

Questions for Self-Evaluation

Use the following questions to gain more clarity:

What Do We Have in Common?

It doesn't come as a shock that alike is pulled into alike. To put it another way, the conventional theory "attracting opposites" is appallingly false.

You may feel drawn to a person that has attributes you don't possess, but in the long run, you're unlikely to be content with them. The variations tend to trigger problems when the attraction and infatuation hormones wear off and gradually tear you apart.

A group of Beijing researchers reported that people tend to collaborate with someone who has a common lifetime focus. Rude Liu, Ran Bian, and colleagues measured the primary motivation of individuals (to meet targets or escape problems), which they described as advancement or protection. They noticed subjects with the same motivation automatically gravitated to men or women.

Do We Have a Strong Physical Connection?

Mutual physical affection in couples contributes to further intimacy and lovemaking, which has been shown to help partners connect and sustain contentment in dedicated relationships.

Meltzer, Makhanova, and colleagues observed that an enjoyable session with a partner helped the pair feel better and increased the marital satisfaction rates up to 48 hours. Overall, partners who make love feel great about the spouse and the relationship most frequently.

Within the couple, the absence of intense sexual desire, vice versa, is linked to a poorer relationship.

How Are We Treating Ourselves and One Another?

- Do you appreciate how one handles you?
- What applies to the way you treat yourself in this relationship?
- Do you appreciate the way you handle your companion or yourself?
- Do you feel satisfied with how you handle your darling?

A stable relationship is one where all these four questions earn a constructive answer. Every couple can have their own ways to arrange themselves and act in a pair, but when all of you are good about it, problems may continue to pop up constantly.

Individuals are mean with each other in certain couples, or one person uses the second person to vent out grievances. Yet they keep thinking, "We really love one another," Loving isn't a real excuse to behave terribly. The problem needs to be addressed.

You, Me, and Us: Is There Stability?

Each relationship has 3 parties: You, your spouse, and the Collective ("Us"). Each of these three entities ought to satisfy the needs. If one person thinks it's all about the partner, then it's a bell of warning. It can be the reverse at times: it's all about "Us" and little consideration of the needs and wishes of each person. It's much more of a concern if there's a sensation that there's no "us."

Do We Contribute Equally?

It's definitely not about making a financial contribution, but putting ongoing and substantial effort into the relationship, which the other person regards as valuable. Often all participants feel as if they are performing all the effort, which suggests they don't consider the second participant's contribution as valuable.

Is the Relationship Reciprocal?

One trend which has been clear over the years, if one person does not want to be in the relationship any longer, it won't survive. Whoever wishes to get out would still consider a problem in what the partner does. Often situations may be restored and patched together if it doesn't fit, but both sides have to show a sincere interest and motivation.

An expert marriage counselor says he essentially knows whether or not a couple has the potential to work things out within the first 5 minutes they come into the session. If the partners sit down on a sofa next to each other, they're offered a chance. Even if they try their utmost to stay as far apart as possible from each other, that's a normal fight that failed.

Do We Have Common Values?

It is impossible to push forward as a unified front until the fundamental principles are compatible. Your values and ideals will continuously collide. For example, if the most important value of one couple is family, but its liberation for the partner, the couple would suffer.

Do We Have Common Goals?

People sometimes initiate a relationship solely based on physical affection and then discover that they want opposite things in life. For example, Russian women online dating people typically want to get married and have babies, but their partners just want something simple with little commitment. These competing objectives are likely to collide, even though shared desire and attraction are present. Many couples begin their lives together desiring the same things, but through the years, their goals shift. Realigning goals and expectations is an important aspect of holding the relationship intact.

Am I a Nice Person Next to My Sweetheart?

Some people are putting the best in us, while some are making the exact opposite impact. When you love this person but don't like who you are in their company, this relationship doesn't do any of you any good. Having a self-destructive spouse has a detrimental impact on one's sense of self-worth.

If I Were to Go for a Partner Today, Would I Pick the Same Person?

It is perhaps the most critical query you need to tackle, offering you a clear idea about whether you can stay or leave. If this query is asked, too many people unwaveringly exclaim, "Gosh, NO!" But they still question if it's worth keeping this relationship.

Dimensions to Self-Evaluate

In reality, that is the problem that we will all continue to pose each day. Evaluation of relationships is part of upkeep; if one day you are unexpectedly unaware of the solution, it won't take that much focus. Hopefully, then we won't have too many people to leave a terrible relationship who were 3–10 years late.

Couples will benefit from learning about how they feel about each other and their relationship right now, regardless of how long they have been together. Setting aside time for weekly check-ins can aid in the prevention of potential issues and the establishment of constructive alternatives.

A married pair may use a variety of methods to assess their success, although there are seven easy-to-understand aspects of interpersonal relationships that can be seen as a starting point. They aren't supposed to address aspects that are unique to a particular relationship, so they do serve as a good starting point for questions.

The seven measurements are described below.

Dimension 1: Playing Together

There's no better way to evaluate a marriage than to ask the partners whether they remember to laugh hard together. Humor and playfulness are essential components of a healthy friendship, and they are plentiful at the start of many. It's awesome if playtime is accidental or planned, as long as it's regenerating, light-hearted, and fun.

Playtime means that you can do whatever you want to each other however the two of you want. As a result, you will not be able to bring up any past or future problems, and you will be able to delegate your burdensome responsibilities. As a couple, they become more lighthearted and happier, and they do well together. It's the way people turn into beautiful children because they don't have time to think about each other.

1. How much of the relationship with your girlfriend is now the same?
2. How much do you surprise your girlfriend with something spontaneous and amusing?

3. Do you set your worries aside while you're playing with your partner?

4. Can you make each other laugh hysterically?

5. May you find yourself entertained under similar circumstances?

Dimension 2: Sharing Dreams

You and your wife should be able to share your feelings on problems that aren't part of your daily lives as a couple. It may be as simple as visualizing oneself in various positions from movies and books. You might even fantasize about what you would do if you were unexpectedly blessed with good fortune.

More realistic principles include how you and your partner can explore potential ambitions, such as when you could go or maybe live when you're older. Exploring such possibilities will contribute to more interesting future encounters, such as daydreaming about something you'd like to change or learn more about. And even though they seem to be outside the realm of imagination, these one-of-a-kind shared insights will deepen our comprehension of each other's inner worlds.

Since they have a relationship ahead of them, new partners often talk of their aspirations. More stable partners also overlook the importance of expanding their horizons. Because you have the positive side of memories, you'll use them to create more future fantasies. Which course is chosen, the couples are dedicated to saying whatever comes to mind without fear of being judged?

1. Can you express your abstract feelings and fantasies with your partner on a regular basis?
2. Do you think your girlfriend is involved in your fantasies?
3. Will you maintain each other's critical and emotional perspectives?
4. Would you allow yourself to follow your career goals instead of putting them on hold?
5. Do you feel comfortable sharing anything off your wish list?

Dimension 3: Trust

Ideally, you and your spouse will have complete faith in each other's innermost thinking and feelings and will be able to speak about virtually everything without fear of criticism, embarrassment, or contempt. When anything bad happens, you turn to each other first and trust in your partner's abilities to listen and support.

And even though circumstances are routine, you still have an emotional and mental encounter, and you're never surprised by the unexpected. You're still ready to put in the work to keep up to date, search and understand, and turn with each other as new thoughts or feelings arise.

A good romantic relationship is built on trust. You're confident in your partner's sincerity, dignity, and accountability for what he or she does. You should still trust that if anything changes in his or her attitude toward you, your partner will let you know right away.

Connection is the most important attribute in this dimension. When your partner is distressed by the relationship, the goal is to avoid becoming angry, emotional, or insulted in order to encourage them to open up. If you react with grace and inspiration, you'll learn more about the secret issues that might be lurking underneath what's being said.

1. Do you feel comfortable sharing your vital thoughts and feelings with your spouse for fear of upsetting them?

2. Do you believe your partner pays attention to your worries while you're concerned about something important?

3. Will you rely on your companion to be there when you need them?

4. Do you think about your girlfriend as a close friend?

5. Do you have faith in your partner to hold your feelings and inner thoughts private?

Dimension 4: Working Together as a Team

If they want to stay emotionally involved, both romantic partners can work together to solve life's challenges and problems. All know that they should both be doing their bit as teammates for everything is being asked of them. They happily step over if the other has a good excuse to step back right away, understanding that the relationship's obligations would smooth out over time.

Some couples plan ahead of time what their specific tasks as team members would be, whilst others choose to swap out much of their positions as they see fit or perform some of them together. In any situation, you're still optimistic that you'll be able to sort out your differences by having your shared objectives in mind.

You can depend on each other without worrying that either of you may not follow through on what you've decided to do.

1. Would you trust your companion to do his or her part when a mission has to be completed?
2. Do you believe your mate follows through with his or her promises?
3. Will you rely on your spouse to let you know whether he or she is reluctant to follow through on a promise?
4. Do you feel at ease when you work together on the distribution of responsibilities and effort?
5. Do you discuss topics while you disagree and come up with new ideas?

Dimension 5: Successful Debaters

All couples experience reciprocal stress as a result of the intimate relationship rationales. These continue to be addressed even when one individual relinquishes control to another, resulting in anger and failure. Partners who choose to transform their disagreements into optimal plans hope to find solutions that can keep them as happy as possible.

About the same way, if you and your partner don't agree with anything, you should both listen carefully to each other's point of view. You know how necessary it is to have your companion's wishes as precious to your core as your own.

Couples that disagree about care, respect, or empathy are much more likely to explore solutions that move them closer to a new reality. It isn't, according to them. Rather, they learn the art of dialogue, knowing that if they are called upon to do so, they would sound and respond like their spouses.

1. Once you find yourself in a conflict in which you are the adversary, all of you choose to remain quiet, allow it some time, and return with a more agreeable mindset.
2. Do you like settling conflicts with your mate on an even footing?
3. When you're in a battle, can you openly refer to your partner's point of view?
4. Do you think your partner can pay attention to your needs and consider them even though they conflict with his or her own?
5. Do the ideas meet all of your expectations?

6. Can you accurately reflect your partner's status if asked?

Dimension 6: Raising a Child with Your Partner

We are not only the generation we are now but also the ages we have ever been. Memories are essentially ways to step back in time and recall who we felt at a certain point in time. As a result, there might be times that your intimate partner considers you to be a parent symbolically. This element of a relationship can be the most difficult for certain couples to negotiate.

Your current interactions with the relationship can trigger conscious or unconscious reactions based on your previous experiences. It's almost difficult not to be influenced by our early memories as we respond to the words, movements, facial expressions, voice intonations, and contact of the individual with whom we share our lives in the present.

Will you like to parent a child in the same manner as your actual partner? Will you have treated the child better if you knew anything about him or her? What aspects of his or her character would you respect or despise? How do you make the child feel loved but also responding in ways that are beneficial to both of you?

1. Do you believe your spouse's traits will make him or her likable if he or she were your own child?
2. Would you sympathize with his plight?
3. Would you want to influence his or her actions?
4. Does he or she seem to be fortunate to have you as a parent?
5. Do you think you'd be capable of doing a good job raising him or her?

From the other side of the equation, this question is the counterpart to the previous one. Your partner would still punish you symbolically, as though he or she was raised as a child. You will see how the way of parenting a child has evolved and how it has affected the behavior of your partner with you through looking at your parents' upbringing.

Parental behavior responses can range from pleasantly pleasing to vehemently insulting. Those responses seem to become worse with time. "You start drinking too much, just like your dad," or "Your mother is unbelievably cheap" are examples of negative comments that may evolve from tolerant and positive responses. You must inform your partner how you feel and that you are feeling "parented" in a manner that exudes rage, discomfort, or isolation. On the other hand, you might like the way your partner cradles you when you're angry or when you're down. It's important that your "parental" habits did not re-wound you in the same way they did while you were a kid. When their spouses remember them, they will replace their emotions with ones that will alleviate their childhood sorrows.

Dimension 7: Would You Want Your Partner to Be Your Child's Parent?

1. Does your wife provide you with supportive assistance while you need significant parental care?
2. Do you believe your companion will provide that for you when you are feeling childish, insecure, and in need of comfort?
3. Is your companion willing to lay his or her own desires behind and be present with you as you ask?
4. Is your counterpart capable of recognizing the difference between symbolically parenting you in a positive way versus making you feel worse?
5. Have you ever wished for your partner to be your parent?

Your responses to these questions may change dramatically with time and with each step of your relationship, so if you review them out regularly, you'll be able to see where you've been, where you're headed as a couple, and any adjustments you need to create.

Evaluating the State of Relationship

Making a choice to marry or remain together is a big step because it comes with a lot of confusion about what will happen next. Below is a list of questions to ask yourself and your spouse as a starting point for a conversation to identify your strengths and identify any future problems. You should think about this as a way to assess the actual state of your relationship, which you can do on your own or, better still, as a partner.

Do You Get into Heated Debates?

- If you do, are you able to prevent conflicts from spinning out of control?
- Would you be willing to reconsider your position and approach the problem critically in order to find a solution?

There's a variety about this one. For certain partners, arguing may be characterized as a four-sentence exchange with some snapping and huffing, while for others, it can only be defined by decibel levels above 60 or the usage of swear words. The ability for one or both of you to break when you think the conversation has devolved into emotionally dangerous territory is important.

It takes self-control and self-awareness to keep conflicts from spiraling out of control. When you're mad, it's difficult to resist tunnel vision, which makes you want to prove your case and battle to the death for it. It's fine to be angry, but it's also necessary to recognize when a dialogue becomes pointless and becomes a power fight. If you can do that and save it from getting worse, you've mastered an important relationship talent.

On the other hand, there are those partners that go out of their way to prevent conflict at all costs. Both partners are treading carefully, fearful of revealing their true feelings. Disagreements are brushed aside, and distance is used to avoid confrontation. Since deep affection and interaction becomes unlikely when strong emotions are pushed to the limit, problems seldom get resolved and often accumulate. Over time, the relationship is likely to become more disengaged and superficial.

The second half in each claim is circling around, and this is when couples can soon get stuck. Circling back entails turning around and solving the issue, whether it's all come crashing down in a heated argument or has been swept away too quickly. It's all-too-easy to begin and end with an apology— "Sorry last night," for example—but not to go back and investigate the roots of the dispute. What is the reason for this? And what purpose? And you're scared that a quarrel could break out. The counterintuitive move is to speak up and discuss the problem in order to put it to bed.

What Are Your Decision-Making Methods?

It is, of course, related to the first point about claims—the tool for resolving dilemmas. However, making decisions is primarily about determining what topics can be debated as a group. It pushes the boundaries and the boundaries: I'm not really concerned with the interior design, and I have no idea what kind of sofa you want. Also, I respect your ability to manage income, and I am trusting in your ability to manage the finances. No, my home life is important to me, and I deserve a seat on the couch; or I'm constantly worried about finances, and we have to sit down and hammer out a plan together.

It's about the content—what kinds of topics we can address as a couple and how we'll have fair, positive discussions—and the process—how we'll have rational constructive discussions. It's all about understanding how you process ideas and make choices—Tom, for example, likes to do a lot of work on big issues and needs time to think things through; he's not a guy you can push to think on his feet.

However, decision-making often entails basic power struggles: do all spouses express their emotions, or does one tend to assume responsibility? Was the decision-making phase relaxed and accessible, or was it fraught with anxiety and walking on eggshells?

Do You Know What Disturbs Your Partner the Most?

It's about learning about each person's emotional wounds and trigger points. Kara recognizes Tom's sensitivity to criticism, and although she doesn't keep her tongue and avoid addressing irritants, she is aware of how she addresses her dissatisfaction in order to avoid aggravating Tom's wounds.

Tom is also aware that Kara is vulnerable to feeling neglected or forgotten. He realizes that this isn't about him but about her, her childhood, and her wiring, and he tries to respond quickly when she's speaking to him because he recognizes how vital it is to her. And he's not resentful about it because he doesn't feel like he's giving in to an urge but rather is thinking of her feelings.

Understanding what your partner is vulnerable to and promising to do your best to avoid walking into each other's relational potholes goes a long way toward building a trustworthy relationship. What you don't want to do is dismiss the other's feelings or argue on which reality is right. Everyone has at least one emotional wound, so as a human, you must be able to quickly discuss these problems, reveal them, and react empathically.

The problem is that you just don't realize what you really want—so your common contact is too limited and corrupted that you can't hold these conversations—or you couldn't figure things out and tell each other what you really want.

Do You Discuss the Future? Are You on the Right Page When It Comes to Your Plans and Goals?

This is a dilemma with two sides. It's about sharing a common understanding of what's important in life—children, and family; jobs and career; and wealth —and how it translates into a good life. It's all about imagination, really: how do you see your perfect day or life? What are your targets, and why are you doing this? Will you look forward, both internally and as a couple, to find out what could happen to you both?

But, once again, honesty is rooted in these discussions: will you communicate your desires and goals without fear of being judged? Can I inquire as to what is most relevant to you, and do you concur?

Are You and Your Partner Compatible in Terms of Individual vs. Couple Time?

It's just about your hopes, wishes, and opinions about how you're always wasting your time. Do I want us to snuggle up on the couch and watch TV together at night, or are you playing with the kids as I finish up any chores or work? Is it okay if I hang out with my friends on Saturday or play soccer with my girls, or if I practice my oboe for an hour every night without making you feel bad or deprived?

Communication is a barrier once again, but there is also agreement about what each of you envisions and desires about your time together and as a couple.

Are You Compatible with Desires for Love and Sex?

Are you both working on it as a front-end issue in the same range, even if it can change over time? This isn't only about libido; it's all about everything you need to feel connected to one another. As one is sexually abused or constantly threatened, a fight for dominance is inevitable. The desire to express what each desire without devolving into a conflict or power fight is, once again, the key to clarification.

Are You a Good Fit for the Job?

Since work is such an important aspect of everyone's lives, it's critical that you're on the same page so that you can work together. Is it okay if Kara continues to throw herself into her job and is often willing to work 12 hours a day, or if Tom tries to take money from the shared bank scheme to start his own company? Is it okay, on the other hand, if Kara views a job as just employment, isn't interested in hustling her way up the corporate stairs, and would rather take a lower salary with less hassle and more time off?

Obviously, this isn't only about the work but rather about the effect it has on downtime, personal life, and finances—in other words, goals.

Are You in Agreement Regarding the Extended Family's Role?

Was it fair for my mother to come over for brunch every Sunday, or for us to go to see my friends every Christmas, or for me to owe my brother money to compensate his lawyer for finalizing his divorce?

It's all about bringing together social traditions and desires to solve problems. Maybe your mother will come for dinner once in a while, but not every week; we can alternate Christmas between our families; you should lend money to your brother, but there would be a cap that we all agree.

Is It Easy for You to Get Along 4ith Your In-Laws?

Another factor is the expectations about the level of activity, such as viewing them on Sundays or holidays and drinking heavily before, after, and after. Why would you want to come together if it's impossible? Is your mother-inlaw a doting grandmother, or is your sister-in-law a drama queen who has always been famous to suck the air out of the room?

Will you express your emotions to your husband, and can he or she have constructive feedback to your mother-in-law or sister without offending them?

Is Your Life Partner Your Best Friend? Do You Feel Physically Secure While You are with Them? Do You Have the Impression that They Really Have Your Back and that You Can Always Rely on Them for Assistance?

Those are maybe the most pressing concerns. The common thread running across all of these questions is the method's consistency with the key issues —the content—but, more specifically, how you're handling them. You'll find a way to solve all the other challenges—the things—if you both feel at ease and that your partner is by your side. But, if not, what's the harm? It's the big boulder around halfway down the road. Any extra therapeutic assistance, even if only momentarily, would have a safe forum to talk about those topics, allowing someone else to raise questions that are too difficult to discuss yourself.

But that's also when you'll need the courage to work out how you really feel, explain your own hopes and desires, and figure out what you really need.

Tips to Be a Good Listener

"You really can't listen? You've heard this phrase pretty much at least once in your lifetime. Maybe only a couple of you learned that from your partner. Communicating is also an essential cornerstone in a secure and safe relationship but communicating requires two elements: talking and listening. Talking is a basic thing that everybody does, but this time the emphasis would be on the listening side. Most people are chatting, so only listening to a little bit. Yet, what does one do to be a great listener? Don't worry! Ten strategies below are to help you be one:

Listen More Often

Telling yourself how to become a good listener? The number one suggestion is to listen more often. You may be the person that always talks and forgets how to listen. It never hurts to lower one's ego for long enough to lengthen one's endurance and only listen to what your companion has to tell. When you teach yourself to listen most frequently, as you converse with your boyfriend or girlfriend, it should come automatically.

Communication Is a Two-Way Street

Communication, as stated earlier, is not one way: whether one talks, the other listens. Those positions are interchanged from time to time. The dispute occurs where certain functions are not at all shared, and only one talks and the other listens. Keep in mind that you should know when to stop talking.

Effective contact will never be accomplished if two people in a relationship do not routinely exchange such positions.

Drop Your Phone

It is important for you to drop your phone while talking to your girlfriend or boyfriend, particularly if this is a significant problem. That means you appreciate the individual talking, and you're all ears on what he or she has to say. This is disrespectful if, during a face-to-face talk, one continues checking the screen or fiddling with his or her phone. Turn your phone into a silent mode to be a better listener because those emails and notifications can wait.

Don't Interrupt

Another significant note is never disturbing the one talking in order to become a good listen. Be all ears to what he or she is telling, and wait until the person is done, then share your thoughts on the issue. His or her opinion is just as important as yours on the topic. This shows rudeness if the person speaking is disrupted. Often people get so interested in the topic that they keep cutting off other persons. If you see yourself related to this, consider holding the horses and making others take turns.

Make Eye Contact

Imagine talking to someone who's never gazing at you or staring at something else but you. It is necessary for a successful listener to create and maintain eye contact. It tells your girlfriend or boyfriend you are really concentrated on the subject. You don't have to look someone in the eye to achieve so; depending on the circumstances; only a quick casual glance would do. Setting up eye contact always gives the individual communicating a clear sense that you are really listening.

Look Out for Subtle Hints

Someone needs to take care of the implicit cues to be a better listener. Often you can wonder why he or she becomes moody afterward for an unexplained cause after having a friendly talk with your partner. Some people also have implicit clues in their expressions, so they don't want to say it clearly. For starters, if your girlfriend communicates that she wants spaghetti for dinner, she might drop hints about it, and if you're not a good listener, you may not be able to pick up those hints. It is necessary for any listener to take note.

Show Enthusiasm

Conversing with someone who demonstrates that he or she is obviously not interested is never a good idea. You can't just lay back and stare at your girlfriend or boyfriend because you want to be a good listener; you have to prove you're excited about it. You may achieve so by starting the dialogue first, whether by searching for opportunities to extend the discussion or by posing questions for follow-up. But if you do not feel like talking, it's best to allow yourself some space and offer your partner a strong message that you're not in the right state to carry an intelligible conversation.

Be Patient

Patience is a virtue and one of the key components of how to become a good listener. To listen, you have to hold a very ample amount of courage within yourself. You'll definitely need it if your partner complains about something that happened in her or his day. Being good at listening helps the individual to take their time to articulate what they want to tell.

If you consider yourself on the restless side, it is highly advised to take deep breaths and set speaking time intervals.

Give a Proper Response

You have to be attentive, too, in order to become a better listener. If just one talks, it's not a good conversation because the other either nods or shakes his or her head. If you're a good listener, you'll be able to respond coherently to any question you're being asked if you listen well. Often a yes or no is not enough to address the subject. Keep an emphasis on participating in the discussion.

Understand What They Say into the Heart

This is the same as eating, and you can't just consume the meal; you need to digest it, too. You can't just listen to what he or she has to say. You have to take it to heart as well. When your companion mentions something that does trouble him or her, you should be vigilant. For example, when you are asked to do the tasks, don't make him or her repeat him or herself; recall what job you were given. It demonstrates you are not only listening but adapting what you learned about your discussions to your relationship as well.

This requires effort and a lot of courage to become a great listener. You don't have to try to be one, but instead encourage yourself to make such changes little by little, particularly if you're not the kind of individual that's used to listening. Communication operates both ways, and you just have to take the patience to speak and listen.

CHAPTER 8

HOW TO MANAGE THOUGHTS TO CONTROL ANXIETY?

When you have an external cut, all you have to do is apply disinfectant to treat it and prevent infection. In time, the wound will close up, and you will be as good as new. How beautiful it will be if you can

address negative thoughts and anxiety-provoking thoughts like this! Addressing negative thoughts that control anxiety is not as straightforward. In addressing negative thoughts, various approaches can help. The good news is that this manual will shed light on the best ways to deal with your thoughts to prevent them from graduating from an anxiety disorder.

One important and helpful way is to make mental shifts. In other words, intentionally adjusting the way you think of challenging an established thought pattern. This happens by changing the way you judge an event or situation. It is a form of training for the brain such that it doesn't succumb to anxiety-generating thoughts.

This is not going to be a straightforward process because it involves "uninstalling" and "deprogramming" many negative behaviors and thinking patterns responsible for anxiety. If, as a little girl, for instance, your dad keeps hammering it that no one will love you if you are fat, it will end up haunting the girl for life. Hence, she might even resort to unhelpful means to try and keep fit.

A mental shift is one guaranteed way to break off the shackles of unhelpful thoughts. This chapter will shed light on unhelpful thinking patterns and how to manage them to control anxiety.

Beware of thoughts that place excessive demands on you. They start with "I" or "should." Many times, these demands are impossible to live up to, which ends up fueling our anxiety. The problem with this sort of thought is the compulsion and pressure it puts on us. When this gets to a level, we end up procrastinating or avoiding what we want to do as a means of escaping. In the long run, this ends up triggering more anxiety.

With this in mind, rather than telling yourself you should do things, think of a kind, calm and gentle approach to keep yourself motivated towards the task before you. You can think of another means without graduating into a negative thought pattern.

8.1 Understanding Cognitive Distortions

In addition to the "Should" form of thinking, other ways negative thoughts express themselves are called cognitive distortions. A few of them are:

Mental Filtering

With mental filtering, the victim only concentrates heavily on the negative side of events. In other words, no matter the bright side of an event, he or she does not care. They are so paralyzed by the negativity that they do not celebrate their achievement. They dwell on this till it triggers anxiety.

For instance, take the case of a married couple where the husband cheated. Even after promising and swearing never to repeat such an act of infidelity, the wife will not let go. She even questions all the years of their marriage, thinking and assume it is all a lie.

Black and White Thinking Pattern

Also known as polarized thinking, this person approaches everything with an all-or-nothing mentality. In other words, humans or circumstances are either perfect or not. They are either the best parent, or they are a failure. This affects their relation and disposition to life in general as no middle ground exists in their world. This explains why this person can easily fall into anxiety and negative thinking pattern when things do not go on the positive side.

Overgeneralization

With this distortion, a person concludes (most times, bad) from a single incident. For instance, a person who once had a terrorist attack at a mall will conclude that malls are places where evil lurks. He or she will do all in their capacity to avoid going to the mall. They expect the terrible event to be a norm that should keep repeating at the mall. This person will, in turn, suffer severe anxiety at the thought of visiting the mall.

Another example is a shy guy that summons the courage to talk to a lady he's had feelings for. Assuming his voice failed him in trying to do this, he could conclude that he sucks and will never try to talk to a lady again. Simply entertaining the thought of trying again could send his heart rating triggering anxiety.

Mind Reading or Jumping to Conclusion

From the name, people in this category assume to know what everyone is thinking. The issue with this is that their assumption is usually negative, which is wrong most times.

For instance, your husband suddenly frowns in the middle of a meal, and you conclude he doesn't like the meal, or it is salty. This assumption makes you sad, triggering anxiety at what could come after. This could, however, be wrong as he could suddenly remember an unpleasant situation that made him uncomfortable.

Personalization

With this distortion, the victim assumes that everything someone else says or does is directly related to them. Everything will be taken personally. As a result, the victim engages in an unhealthy comparison for the best, smartest, or brightest.

The sad part is that this person takes the blame for unpleasant things that has no link to them. For instance, "If I had stayed at home, Tom would have studied for his exam and passed." This makes the person sink into a pattern of unhealthy thoughts which could trigger anxiety.

Fallacy of Fairness

In an ideal world, everyone is happy; things go smoothly because the world is governed by an unseen rule of right or wrong. Unfortunately, however, this does not happen, which could make some people feel bad when confronted with the unpleasant parts of life. This person fails to realize that life is not fair, and things will not always go our way.

This person lives life, assuming that everything would be fair. However, when life events and circumstances disobey this rule, the person ends up with negative thoughts, which could cause anxiety.

8.2 How to Control Negative Thoughts to Beat Anxiety?

Every blessed day, humans battle with unwanted thoughts: "How could I be so stupid?" "I will never learn," "I cannot seem to do anything right," etc. We place such high demands on ourselves, and our minds succumb to such negative thoughts. In return, it triggers anxiety, worry, doubt, and a feeling of unworthiness. The worst case is that this negative thought makes a cycle that keeps repeating itself over and over.

The good news is that there are many positive steps you can take to have a turnaround and break free of the cycle of thoughts that causes anxiety. You can come up with a viable strategy to counter those thoughts to prevent anxiety. This section explores how you can control negative thoughts:

Turn Negative to Positive Action

Should you be bewildered by an obsessive thought that's calling you to do something, listen to the dictate of that thought and attend to it. In the same way, you will not ignore the check engine light of your vehicle forever. No matter how hard you try to avoid looking at it, it is right before you every time you are driving. You will not, because of the check engine light, discard the vehicle or give it out. In the same manner, should thought be a cry for help, do not ignore it.

In other words, take a break and attend to the situation. If you feel scared and tensed to the extent of triggering anxiety, for instance, take a break and consider what is making you scared. Rather than pushing the feeling away, take some time off and examine why you are scared as well as looking for how to address it.

Once you are calm enough to deal with the matter, come up with an action plan. By this, we mean positive and actionable steps that can help. Doing this should address the real source of the anxiety rather than trying to push the thoughts away.

Avoid Indulging in the Level of Futility

In dealing with unhelpful thoughts, there is a tendency to keep doing what doesn't work. However, the problem is evident –

they never work. The issue is because of how easy it is easy for the brain to succumb to these useless tactics over and over.

With this in mind, rather than falling back to self-defeating thoughts, consider another approach. It is not about fighting old habits but noticing what doesn't work and sticking to what works.

Expand Your Awareness

A constricted mind is like a tight muscle. The degree of movement will be very limited. A few of the things that constrict the mind are old beliefs, inertia, habits, fear, low expectations, and old conditioning. You, however, need to confront this with all honesty.

A closed mindset does no good. With this in mind, on detecting any inner discomfort, be sure to expand your awareness. For instance, a feeling of hatred towards your neighbor is a clear example of a contracted mindset. With an open mindset, however, you can tolerate the person, see another good side of them rather than seeking out their fault.

Combat Shades of Green Thinking

Our mind has been conditioned to taking the easy way out. In thinking and making decisions, we love the easy way as it speeds our progress and helps our decision-making. This is about dealing with black and white thinking patterns, which could be challenging as it holds the person to irrational beliefs.

Rather than getting anxious with shades of gray thought, we recommend evaluating circumstances on a scale of 0 to 10. Falling short of expectations should be seen as a partial failure, rather than sinking into anxiety and beating yourself up.

For instance, someone could say, "I am very useless; I could not wake up to go over my notes for this evening's exam." However, how sure are you that missing a single morning will affect your chance of success? When you analyze this on a scale, it could be a 7% likelihood. This helps the anxiety of looking at the circumstance in terms of complete failure.

See Disappointments as Part of Life

You might not be able to do much about disappointments. With this in mind, condition your mind to expect them once in a while. Avoid thinking too much of people and circumstances so that should things go in a way you didn't like; the blow will not be too much. Life will throw a lot at you. Bear in mind that your reactions to all the happenings have a lot to do with your wellbeing. You can either sink into anxiety or rise above it, seeing it as part of life.

It is vital to know the difference between the things you can control and the ones you cannot. It takes a wise man to let go of things he cannot control. This is the secret to happiness and rising above anxiety that comes with disappointments. You were jilted despite your faithfulness and dedication to the relationship. It hurts, we know, but mourn it and move forward, preparing yourself for the next available partner.

What to do when anxiety and depression come back.

The following methods will help you overcome anxiety and depression.

Acknowledge that Thoughts Emerge Normally

If you cannot change them, then try working to supplant them with other "better" thoughts. Try not to pummel yourself over something you cannot control, but do not overlook them either; basically, move past them and decide not to relate to them, even as they cloud your mind.

8.3 Building an Unwavering Intention to Save Yourself

A commitment to yourself is a vow you decide to keep for good and not break no matter what happens. The commitment to fight depression means vowing never to give in to the problem, standing up for yourself, and committing not to pay heed to all the negative thoughts/suggestions/ideas that keep perturbing you.

By building this commitment, you tell yourself that from now onwards, you will make a conscious effort to safeguard your sanity, see things from a positive perspective, avoid overthinking things, stay in the present, and fight routine stress before it morphs into chronic stress, anxiety, and depression. This commitment reminds you of your promise to protect yourself from undue worry and tension and stay normal whenever you start to overgeneralize things and pay too much attention to trivial things. This commitment encourages you to follow the different techniques and remedies that help you battle depression and live a happy, calm life.

After building the intention to be depression-free, your next step is to practice the remedies we shall discuss shortly. Before moving on to those, let us find out how you can build this unwavering commitment.

8.4 Exercise

Exercise is a highly recommended stress reliever for many reasons. Physical activity has many benefits in addition to reducing stress, and these benefits alone (increased health, longevity, and happiness) make exercise a worthwhile habit. And as a stress management technique, it is more effective than others. The combined benefits of these two facts make physical exercise a lifestyle that is worth following.

Do Physical Activity

The definition of physical activity in this context has not been limited only to exercise. Physical activity is any activity that engages your physique. Mostly it will lead to perspiration. When an individual engages in physical activity, he or she is obliged to concentrate fully on that particular activity. Exercising is a very renowned way to counter depression. Regular exercise has time and again been used as an anti-depressant. When one is exercising, endorphins are boosted. These are chemicals that enable an individual to feel good.

The statistics of how many people deal with stress are always on the upward. When one experiences stress, it has a lasting effect on their life since it cuts across what an individual is engaging in at a particular time. To eradicate stress completely is an uphill task, and one would rather manage it. Exercising is one of the best methods to manage stress. Many medical practitioners advise that individuals should engage in exercises in a bid to manage stress levels.

The advantages that come with a person engaging in exercises have far been established to be a countermeasure against diseases and as a method of enhancing the body's physical state. Research has it that exercising helps a great deal when decreasing fatigue and enhancing the body's consciousness of the environment. Stress invades the whole of your body, affecting both the body and mind. When this happens, the act of your mind feeling well will be pegged on the act of the body feeling well too. When one is in the act of exercising, the brain produces endorphins that act naturally as pain relievers. They also improve the instances upon which an individual falls asleep. When the body is able to rest, this means that its amounts of anxiety have dropped by a large margin. Production of endorphins can also be triggered by the following practices. They include but are not limited to meditation and breathing deeply. Participation in exercise regularly has proven an overall tension reliever.

8.5 Doing Relaxation Exercises

Another method of reducing stress levels is through the use of some relaxation techniques. A relaxation technique is any procedure that is of aid to an individual when trying to calm down the levels of anxiety. Stress is effectively conquered when the body itself is responding naturally to the stress levels in the body. Relaxation can often be confused with laying on a couch after a hard day. This relaxation is best done in the form of selfmeditation, although its effects are not fulfilling on the impact of stress. Most relaxation techniques are done at the convenience of your home with only an app.

The following types of exercise are highly recommended for stress reduction because they have specific properties that are effective in reducing stress in short and long-term stress management: Yoga.

The gentle stretching and balance of yoga may be what people think when they practice, but there are several other aspects of yoga that help reduce stress and to have a healthy life. Yoga entails the same type of diaphragmatic breathing; this is used with meditation. In fact, a few yoga styles include meditation as part of their practice (in fact, most types of yoga can take you to some degree of meditation).

Yoga also includes balance, coordination, stretching, and styles are the exercise of power. All support health and stress reduction. Yoga can be practiced in many ways. Some yoga styles feel like a gentle massage from the inside, while others sweat and hurt you the next day, so there is a yoga school that can work for most people, even for those who have some physical limitations, to be attractive.

Walking

Walking is one of the easiest medications to relieve stress that is excellent because of the benefits this technique offers. The human body was designed to travel long distances, and this activity generally did not cause as much wear as it did. Walking is an exercise that can be easily separated by the speed you use, the weights you carry, the music you listen to, and the location and the company you choose.

This type of exercise can also be easily divided into 10 minutes of sessions, and classes are not needed, and no special equipment is needed beyond a good pair of shoes. (This is an advantage since studies have shown that three 10-minute workouts provide the same benefits as a 30minute session: great news for those who, due to their busy schedule, need to practice in parts! To find the More smalls!)

Martial Arts

There are many forms of martial arts, and although each one may have little focus, ideology, or set of techniques, they all have benefits to relieve stress. These practices tend to pack both aerobic and strength training, as well as the confidence that comes from physical and self-defense skills.

Generally practiced in groups, martial arts can also offer some of the benefits of social support, as classmates encourage each other and maintain a sense of group interaction. Many martial arts styles provide philosophical views that promote stress management and peaceful life, which you can choose or not accept. However, some styles, especially those with high levels of physical combat, have a higher risk of injury, so martial arts are not for everyone, or at least not all styles work for everyone. If you try several different martial arts programs and talk to your doctor before following the style, you have a better chance of finding a new habit that keeps you fit for decades.

These three examples are not the only types of exercise. They simply show some benefits and are usable by most people. There are many other forms of working out that can be very powerful, such as Pilates, running, weight training, swimming, dancing, and prepared sports.

Everyone brings their stress management benefits to the table, so discover and practice the form of exercise that appeals to you the most.

Mindfulness Body Scan Meditation

This technique requires a more formal atmosphere than the breathing technique, as it is best experienced when you are lying down or sitting in a really comfortable posture. While lying down may seem like a fabulous way, initially, it might not be a good idea in the long run because novices tend to fall asleep in this position. Also, while a good 30-minute duration is needed for effective results, you may make the best use of whatever little time you get.

Sit down on a cushion or a chair or lie down comfortably on the floor. Avoid lying on a mattress if you find it difficult to stay awake. Close your eyes because it makes it easy to focus. Now, pay attention to your breath. Slowly move your attention to the places where your body is in contact with your chair or floor. Investigate each section of your body mentally.

The different sensations you experience could be tingling, pressure, tightness, temperature, or anything else. Sometimes, you may not feel any sensation too. Notice the absence of sensations also. Each section of your body becomes an anchor for your mind to hold on to so that it doesn't wander away.

Again, be aware when your mind wanders, and gently get it back to where it was before it moved off. When you are done, open your eyes and mindfully get your focus back on the outside environment.

Another crucial aspect of the body scan mindfulness technique is to release the tension in the various parts of your body as you scan it. When you focus on a particular section of the body, say your shoulders, you suddenly realize that you are holding them too rigid and creating tension in that area. By focusing on that part, tension is automatically released from there.

These are formal ways of body scans and breathing mindfulness meditation techniques. You can do these mindfulness activities even while sitting in your chair in your office. Take a 5-minute break and do a body scan or focus on your breath even as you sit at your desk. You don't even have to get up from your seat.

Also, you could do it during your daily commute or while waiting for someone or standing in line for something or anywhere else.

CONCLUSION

There are several sources of anxiety, and depending on the degree of the condition, there are also many different therapies available. The easiest approach to consult a psychiatrist is that a combination of therapies can

be developed by the therapist or psychologist, ranging from medicine, counseling, methods of self-care, relaxation exercises, etc. By measuring the degree of your anxiety, they do this and, thus, prescribe the appropriate therapies. Meditation is one of the pillars of rehabilitation at nearly all stages. Meditation is, in no shape or type, it may be a main anxiety medication. It is a complementary therapy with advantages that reach well beyond what has been demonstrated by medicine and study.

You actually break down harmful thoughts or stimuli, anxiety, and concern by meditation. You also rely mindfully on the sensations and acknowledge what you can manage and what you cannot.

I hope you think about these meditations if you ever go through a tough time and take a few minutes for yourself. Even if you have just a few minutes, a gentle breathing meditation will help you bring it all into perspective. Know that the longer you exercise, the more your peace of mind gets greater. I hope you've loved practicing anxiety meditation. Now move ahead to lead your very best life.

www.ingramcontent.com/pod-product-compliance
Lightning Source LLC
Chambersburg PA
CBHW050019130526
44590CB00042B/958